T&T CLARK STUDY GUID

THE GOSPEL ACCORDING TO MATTHEW

Series Editor
Tat-siong Benny Liew, College of the Holy Cross, USA

Other titles in the series include:

1&2 Thessalonians: An Introduction and Study Guide
1 Peter: An Introduction and Study Guide
2 Corinthians: An Introduction and Study Guide
Colossians: An Introduction and Study Guide
Ephesians: An Introduction and Study Guide
Galatians: An Introduction and Study Guide
James: An Introduction and Study Guide
John: An Introduction and Study Guide
Luke: An Introduction and Study Guide
Mark: An Introduction and Study Guide
Matthew: An Introduction and Study Guide
Philemon: An Introduction and Study Guide
Philippians: An Introduction and Study Guide
Romans: An Introduction and Study Guide
The Acts of the Apostles: An Introduction and Study Guide
The Letters of Jude and Second Peter: An Introduction and Study Guide

T&T Clark Study Guides to the Old Testament:

1 & 2 Samuel: An Introduction and Study Guide
1 & 2 Kings: An Introduction and Study Guide
Ecclesiastes: An Introduction and Study Guide
Exodus: An Introduction and Study Guide
Ezra-Nehemiah: An Introduction and Study Guide
Hebrews: An Introduction and Study Guide
Leviticus: An Introduction and Study Guide
Jeremiah: An Introduction and Study Guide
Job: An Introduction and Study Guide
Joshua: An Introduction and Study Guide
Psalms: An Introduction and Study Guide
Song of Songs: An Introduction and Study Guide
Numbers: An Introduction and Study Guide

MATTHEW: AN INTRODUCTION AND STUDY GUIDE

Basileia of the Heavens is Near at Hand

By
Elaine M. Wainwright
With
Robert J. Myles and Carlos Olivares

Bloomsbury T&T Clark
An imprint of Bloomsbury Publishing Plc

B L O O M S B U R Y
LONDON • OXFORD • NEW YORK • NEW DELHI • SYDNEY

Bloomsbury T&T Clark
An imprint of Bloomsbury Publishing Plc

Imprint previously known as T&T Clark

50 Bedford Square
London
WC1B 3DP
UK

1385 Broadway
New York
NY 10018
USA

www.bloomsbury.com

First published 2017

British Library Cataloguing-in-Publication Data
A catalogue record for this book is available from the British Library.

ISBN: PB: 978-1-3500-0879-3
ePDF: 978-1-3500-0881-6
ePub: 978-1-3500-0880-9

Library of Congress Cataloging-in-Publication Data
A catalog record for this book is available from the Library of Congress.

Series: T&T Clark Study Guides to the New Testament, volume 1

Cover design: clareturner.co.uk

Typeset by Newgen Knowledge Works (P) Ltd., Chennai, India
Printed and bound in Great Britain

This volume is dedicated to doctoral students who become colleagues in our discipline and in particular to Drs Robert J. Myles and Carlos Olivares who have collaborated very significantly in this production from beginning to end.

My deepest gratitude

CONTENTS

Introduction

And the child shall be called Emmanuel,
a name which means 'God is with us'.

Paraphrase of Mt. 1.23b

As you begin to read this Guide to the Gospel of Matthew, you are invited to take up into your hands and read in print or now also on a computer screen the text of the Gospel according to Matthew. To do so is to encounter a classical text. We can feel the touch of the text in our hands and our eyes see it and read it through the material matter of the text or computer. Engaging the Gospel of Matthew is a sensuous act that brings us into contact with the materiality of this text in its myriads of manifestations on papyri, vellum, paper, as manuscript and as book and more recently as digital text. As well as this material history, The Gospel according to Matthew has also had a long history of sociality into which we are invited as we take up the text. Its initial author/s were not only engaged with the papyri of the text, their writing instruments and their ink but also the life of a human community telling the story of Jesus, a story which was shaping their lives in their geographical, socio-political and religio-cultural contexts. Similar experiences of materiality and sociality have accompanied this Gospel story down through its history as it has been translated into myriads of languages, as it has shaped and been shaped by the emerging Christian traditions in multiple new locations, and as it has been received and lived by individuals and communities of faith and as it has been studied by scholars. We are caught up into all of this richness as we begin to read and to study this Gospel (Elvey 2011: 44-67).

As authors of this Guide, we have cited as its opening words Mt. 1.23: 'And the child shall be called Emmanuel, a name which means "God with us"'. This verse functions with Mt. 28.20 as a frame around this Gospel's story of Jesus, and this frame shapes meaning. In the child to be born of Mary, the narrator proclaims, divinity has entered not only into human history but also into Earth's history—divinity is, in this child, with 'us' as Earth community (not only human but other-than-human) in our multifaceted unfolding. At the end of the Gospel, Jesus who has been raised by the power of this same divinity promises to stay with 'us', the Earth community, to the end of the ages. Within this framework, the evangelist offers readers many other indicators or signs for shaping one's reading, for understanding, for making meaning of this Gospel text. The explicit programmatic, which characterizes the life of Jesus portrayed in the Gospel of Matthew is his opening proclamation which echoes that of John the Baptist: repent for the *basileia* [kin(g)dom] of the heavens is near at hand (Mt. 3.2; 4.17). It is this which we have chosen for the sub-title of this Guide.

As you, the reader of this Guide, take up this text, our invitation to you is that you first read and engage with the classical text with which it is concerned, namely the Gospel according to Matthew. Read the Matthean Gospel as a narrative—seek to read it/to hear it as if you have never read or heard it before. Listen for its repetitions, look for its shape, its sense, its emphases and key concerns. You will then be in a better position to engage with Chapter 1 of the Guide that lays out the unfolding narrative that is called the Gospel according to Matthew. Some key headings will facilitate your recognizing its patterns, nuances and emphases.

Having engaged the Matthean text or the Matthean narrative, you will then better understand the ways in which we have chosen to guide you into further understanding the Gospel. One pathway that we will open up for you is that of some of the currents within recent Matthean scholarship. We can introduce you only to a selection of the contemporary biblical scholars who are seeking in various ways to understand and to explicate the Matthean story of Jesus, in all its complexity. Along this pathway, we will limit our purview to material appearing from the mid 1990s up to the present.

We have chosen this particular timeframe for a number of reasons but predominantly because this is the period that has not yet been included in any introductory guide to Matthew's Gospel. This book has, therefore, its precursors whose content we do not propose to repeat here. You would do well, therefore, to take these others in hand with this volume as you seek to introduce yourself to Matthean scholarship. The first precursor is Donald Senior's *What Are They Saying about Matthew* that was published by Paulist Press in 1983. It covered the period from the emergence of redaction criticism into English-speaking scholarship in the 1960s up to the early 1980s. This was the period in which redaction criticism as a method or tool within the historical critical methodology was at its peak and the sections into which Senior divides the literature he surveys reflect this dominant approach: setting, sources and structure together with use of the Old Testament; and then the key theological themes which were emerging—salvation history, law, christology and church.

In 1996, Senior produced 'A Revised and Expanded Edition' of his overview of scholarship under the same headings with one difference—his last chapter title was expanded to include 'Discipleship' with 'Church'. In his preface, he drew attention to the shifts in methodological approaches that had characterized the period of a little over a decade since his previous edition. These included a range of new literary critical approaches together with the social-scientific approach. In reading this new edition, you not only gain an overview of Matthean scholarship to the early eighties but this is supplemented by that which emerged in the subsequent period up to the mid-1990s under the same subject headings. It is of interest to note that a bibliography has been added to the second edition and it contains an almost equal number of entries dated prior to 1983 and subsequent to 1983. Page numbers have increased from eighty-five to one hundred and thirty-six.

Alongside Senior's guide(s) to Matthean scholarship as a way of understanding the Gospel stands John Riches, *Matthew*, in the New Testament Guides series published by Sheffield Academic Press, also in 1996. It is the precursor of this volume and together with Senior's 1996 edition of *What are They Saying about Matthew* should be pre-reading for this work. In his opening chapter, Riches raises what he considers the 'leading questions' (theological, literary and historical) in Matthean scholarship in the mid 1990s. These lead him to explore the literary aspects of the Matthean Gospel: its sources especially as understood according to the two-source theory, and its literary characteristics. His second chapter locates the Gospel within its first-century context, and then delineates the range of opinions as to its geographic location, its relation to Judaism and its place within emerging Christianity of the first century. In his final chapter, Riches provides an overview of current Matthean scholarship that focuses on the central question of Christology.

In this current volume in the series Phoenix Guides to the New Testament, we intend to supplement these two prior works by renowned Matthean scholars, not to repeat them. Our emphases will, therefore, be threefold. First, we have already invited you into reading the Gospel text as it is this narrative that we seek to understand. The first chapter will provide a guide to reading the text, pointing to the different text markers, narrative features and other storytelling devices that shape meaning. We suggest, however, that you keep the text of the Gospel near when reading the remaining chapters also as the work of the scholars to whom we will introduce you has as its goal a deeper understanding of the Gospel text. Indeed, it is helpful to develop the habit as a biblical scholar of always reading explanations of the Gospel text with the Gospel in hand.

This brings us to the second emphasis of this volume alluded to above: namely, an introduction to both recent scholars of the Gospel and the particular thematics or narrative trends that they see emerging from their particular readings of the Gospel. This material will unfold in Chapters 2 to 4. It will be interwoven, however, with the third emphasis chosen for this Guide: we want to introduce you to the particular methodology or methodologies used by recent Matthean scholars in undertaking their interpretations of the text together with the interpretive lens (or hermeneutic) that they utilize. Both of these shape the particular meaning/s that scholars make of the Gospel and so as you are introduced to them and their work, we will seek to keep them linked closely with the texts they are interpreting. We invite you therefore to keep your Gospel text in hand so that coming to know the Matthean scholars and their ways of reading facilitates a deeper understanding of the Matthean narrative.

In a final chapter, Chapter 5, we will demonstrate how a contemporary hermeneutical perspective—namely, the ecological—can be combined with careful attention to methodology to read a familiar Matthean text: the Beatitudes. The bibliography provided will advance the one provided in Senior's second edition and the reading lists at the end of each of Riches' chapters.

We are grateful to Professor Tat-siong Benny Liew of The College of the Holy Cross (USA) for the invitation to prepare this Guide to the Gospel of Matthew. It provided the opportunity for collaboration between an established scholar in Matthean Studies and two colleagues who were doctoral students at the time of our beginning the undertaking and who were and are themselves conducting ground-breaking scholarship in the field. Such collaboration is one of the highlights of our academic work. Our hope is that this Guide, by reviewing current scholarship in the field and pointing to new and emerging areas, will open up the Gospel of Matthew to a new generation of Matthean scholars.

Chapter 1

Reading the Matthean Narrative

'The book of the genealogy...' (Mt. 1.1).

The Gospel of Matthew begins with these words: 'The book of the genealogy of Jesus Christ, son of David, son of Abraham' (Mt. 1.1). They stand as a caption for the Gospel as a whole as well as for the genealogy that follows in 1.2-17. They also introduce readers to the focal character—Jesus—and name him as *Christos*, son of David and son of Abraham. The reader is left in no doubt, from the outset, that this *biblos* or 'book' is not only about a Jewish protagonist (Jesus), but that he and his story will also be located firmly within Jewish traditions and practices. More than that, however, the opening phrase, 'book of the genealogy', evokes intertextually the book of the genealogy of the heavens and the earth of Gen. 2.4a as well as that of the human community, male and female, of Gen. 5.1-2. And while the Matthean author may have had a different cosmology from ours today, the story of Jesus is located in the unfolding story of the heavens and earth [the Universe] and the human community.

Genesis/Birth

Genesis or 'birth' characterizes the first chapter of the narrative and links it to the second. Thirty-nine times the listener to the Matthean storytelling hears the phrase, 'male/father *gave birth to* male/son (1.2-16), drawing on traditions from the Jewish scriptures as well as other literary sources available to the community. Hence, Jesus' story is linked intimately with that of the Jewish nation and carries the claim that God is at work in this birth as God has been at work in the unfolding story of community and cosmos evoked by the genealogy. The dominant narrative is andro- or male-centric but the naming of four women in the genealogy—Tamar (1.3), Rahab (1.5), Ruth (1.5) and 'the wife of Uriah' (i.e. Bathsheba, 1.6), together with Mary 'of whom Jesus, was born' in the concluding verse (1.16)—introduces a tensive note into the narrative, the first of many not only associated with gender but also with power, authority, community structures and many other issues. And often these tensions are simply allowed to remain in the Matthean narrative, as in the genealogy and birth narrative, without being resolved. As such they may well be indicative of similar tensions, without resolution, that characterized the community at the time of the writing of the Gospel.

Matthew 1.16 is a problematic verse in that it ought to close off the genealogy of 1.2-16 climactically but, in fact, it breaks things wide open because Jesus is not born of Joseph but of Mary. Discontinuity together with continuity constitute the beginning of the Matthean story of Jesus, and spill over into 1.18-24, where the evangelist theologizes the pregnancy of Mary outside of her betrothal to Joseph. Continuing this theologizing, the narrative constructs the child, Jesus, as a savior figure like Joshua and Moses and, by way of the first 'fulfillment text' of Isa. 7.14, introduces a theme that will span the narrative: God is with 'us', the Earth/human communities evoked in 1.1, in this child, Jesus. In the final verse of the Gospel, Jesus, who has been raised by this same God, promises to be with the Gospel community (an Earth/human community) to the end of the ages (Mt. 28.20). In the language of scholars, the Gospel is framed by God being with the human/Earth community in the person of Jesus, whose story is just beginning to unfold in the opening chapter.

The first verse of Matthew 2 continues to draw out the narrative thread of birth, noting that Jesus was born in Bethlehem in Judea. This birth, like that of Roman emperors and other prestigious figures in the period, was characterized by cosmic phenomena. In this instance, a star leads visitors from the East to Jerusalem to find the child whose birth the star heralded. The encounter between Herod and the visitors with its intrigue and deception opens the way for the initial withdrawal of Jesus by Joseph in the face of political threat (2.13-14), a theme that will characterize the unfolding Matthean story of Jesus (2.12, 13, 14, 22; 4.12; 12.15; 14.13; 15.21). The two introductory chapters close on this note as Joseph withdraws with the child and his mother to Nazareth in Galilee to avoid the tyranny of Archelaus, Herod's son. The story of Jesus is immersed in the political intrigue of first-century Palestine on the edges of the Roman Empire as much as it is grounded in the Jewish sacred story. The tensive note that echoes out from Matthew 2 with its theme of escape or withdrawal is this: why was the divine intervention only on behalf of Jesus, and not all the children of Bethlehem?

Preachers of the Basileia

A significant shift in time to the days of John the Baptist preaching in the wilderness of Judea (3.1) seems to suggest that Matthew 1–2 provides an introduction to the Gospel, which can be seen as structured into five 'books', each characterized by narrative (Matthew 3–4; 8–9; 11–12; 14–17; 19–23) and discourse blocks (Matthew 5–7; 10; 13; 18; 24–25), with each of the second group being marked off by a formula at its end: 'when Jesus had finished…' (7.28; 11.1; 13.53; 19.1 and 26.1). These are framed by the Infancy Narrative (Matthew 1–2) and the Passion Narrative (Matthew 26–28). There are, however, other narrative and structural features woven into the text that suggest different structures. Matthew 4.17 and 16.21 both begin with the phrase '[f]rom that time Jesus began to…', suggesting that the Jesus story consists of his Galilean ministry and his journey to Jerusalem together with his ministry there leading into his death. A number of scholars using narrative criticism suggest slightly different structures. It remains clear, however, that the life and ministry of Jesus as narrated in this Gospel is characterized by preaching, teaching and healing (4.23; 9.35) and that this takes place in both Galilee and Jerusalem with a turn in the narrative occurring around the Caesarea Philippi incident in Mt. 16.13-20. As you read the Gospel text, you might watch for those characteristics that indicate the narrative structure that the Matthean storyteller wishes to give to the Gospel and how this has been encoded into the text.

In Matthew 3–4, as the ministry 'baton' is passed from John the Baptist to Jesus, the reader discovers the key characterization of Jesus' ministry in Matthew. Both prophetic figures proclaim: 'Repent, for the *basileia* of the heavens is near at hand' (3.2; 4.17), a feature that occurs only in Matthew's Gospel. The proclamation of the *basileia*—that is, 'kin[g]dom' or 'empire'—of the heavens is a radical challenge to the *basileia* or 'empire' of Rome that dominates the context in which Jesus preaches this message. The designator, 'of the heavens', sets up a contrast to the *basileia* of Rome: Jesus is preaching an alternative to Rome. The use of 'the heavens' functions in a twofold way: first, it points to this alternative *basileia* being shaped according to the desires of God, who is associated with the realm of the heavens; second, the *ouranos* or 'heaven' can refer to the sky and is intimately linked with 'earth' in repeated phrases like 'heaven/sky and earth' in the Matthean storytelling (5.18; 6.10; 11.25; 16.19; 18.18-19; 23.9; 28.18). At the heart of the Matthean story of Jesus, therefore, is the proclamation of an alternative *basileia*, one that will be characterized by justice and right ordering in accordance with the desires of the God of Jesus. This right ordering includes the Earth and not only the human community, as the language of the Gospel indicates.

Prior to Jesus taking up the ministry from John, however, the reader is alerted to the danger that awaits him. Matthew 4.12 notes, almost in passing, that Jesus heard that John had been arrested. This is followed, however, by the first strategic withdrawal of Jesus, as an adult: he withdraws from the lower regions of the Jordan to Galilee, the place to which Joseph withdrew the child and his mother when he discovered that Archelaus was governing in Judea. Despite this threat, and before Jesus begins explicitly to take up his preaching ministry, he calls others around him—initially Peter and Andrew, James and John (4.18-22).

Preaching, Teaching and Healing

In the first discourse of Jesus (Matthew 5–7) the reader encounters his teaching and preaching of the *basileia* (4.23). The sermon opens with the beatitudes, a text which will be read in more detail in Chapter 5 of this Guide. It is wisdom teaching from the wise teacher/preacher: beatitudes (5.1-12), antitheses (5.21-48), exhortations throughout, and the contrasting of the wise and foolish (7.24-27). This teaching is intimately linked with healing as the narrative shifts to a collection of ten healing stories in Matthew 8–9 and as the entire five chapters (Matthew 5–9) are framed by the parallel texts of Mt. 4.23 and Mt. 9.35. The healing narratives in the Matthean storytelling are, for the most part, abbreviated when compared with the parallel texts in the Gospel of Mark. They are structured into three groups of three (the first healing narrative in the third group has the story of the woman with a haemorrhage intercalated into that of the ruler's daughter so that they become one narrative). There are two buffer pericopes between the groups that combine narrative and teaching. It is here in these chapters that the reader is drawn into the world of corporeality as bodies touch (8.3, 15; 9.20, 29) and healing takes place. As this narrative section draws to a close there is a brief phrase that can be said to characterize Jesus the healer: 'when he saw the crowds, he had compassion on them' (9.36). The Greek verb used here (*splangchnizomai*) is strong: it is to be moved in the depths of one's being, one's entrails, one's innermost parts. This is what characterizes Jesus' healing activity in the Matthean narrative.

Commissioning to Preach, Teach, and Heal

Having been presented to readers of Matthew's Gospel as preacher, teacher and healer in Matthew 5–9, Jesus then commissions 'twelve disciples' to take up those tasks, most explicitly that of preaching and healing, at the beginning of the missionary discourse of Matthew 10. That Jesus is presented as naming twelve disciples to constitute the new kinship group engaged with his mission further evokes the embeddedness of Jesus within Israel's sacred story. The twelve are representative of the twelve tribes of Israel (see the explicit statement in 19.28), a structure through which God has been at work in the past. They, therefore, function symbolically by way of their number, but their mission is concrete: they are sent to preach and heal, the preaching being constituted in the same way as that of John the Baptist and Jesus—namely, the *basileia* of the heavens (10.7). Beyond the initial verses, the mission discourse of Matthew 10 gathers together a range of teachings to guide those sharing with Jesus in a *basileia* ministry but there is no subsequent narrating of their going on mission or returning. This discourse would seem to be directed more to the community shaping this

Gospel; they were continuing the explicit task undertaken by Jesus himself by preaching repentance associated with the *basileia* of the heavens being near at hand. Some contemporary readers might note the absence of women from this commissioned group.

Opposition Mounts as the Mission Unfolds

Diverse narrative units constitute Matthew 11–12. The deeds of Jesus identify him as *Christos* (11.2) and Sophia/Wisdom (11.19). But his deeds also attract the ire of other teachers within first-century Judaism (the Pharisees), and they plot together 'how to destroy him' (12.14). The reader here encounters a theme which has already echoed through Matthew 2 and which will develop as the story unfolds to reach a climax point in the passion narrative. There is mounting opposition to Jesus, the Jewish preacher, and his ministry from the teachers/leaders within the political and religious echelons of his people.

As with Jesus' proclamation from the mountain (Matthew 5–7), so too for the next discourse, the physical location is crucial. Jesus sits beside the Sea of Galilee, the body of water around which so much of his ministry took place. As the mountain on which he sat in 5.1 authorized his teaching, so too now does the boat on the edge of the sea—the material, the social and the sacred are intimately intertwined. From this location, Jesus preaches the *basileia* of the heavens in parables or metaphoric stories about a sower, weeds among wheat, leaven, a mustard seed. Jesus the teacher teases the imagination of his audience to enable them to understand this new way of being that he is calling the *basileia* of the heavens. And the images pile up one upon another. As listeners, we too are confronted by the question Jesus poses to his disciples: 'have you understood all this' (13.51)? The Gospel asks us if we can so readily respond with the disciples: 'Yes!' (13.51). Some scholars see this parable discourse as climactic in the unfolding narrative or as a turning point. However we think of it structurally, it surely is the crucible of Jesus' preaching of the *basileia*; with metaphors and parables, it challenges readers/hearers of this Gospel down through the ages to the repentance that the preaching of the *basileia* of the heavens calls forth.

A long narrative section stretches from Mt. 13.53 to 17.27. The offense that Jesus' own home community takes at him (13.53-58) opens this section; it is then followed by the death of John the Baptist, which John's disciples relay to Jesus (14.1-12). At the close of this section, we hear Jesus making a second prediction that he will face suffering and death (17.22-23; cf. 16.21). Opposition to Jesus is mounting but he is not deterred in his task of proclaiming the *basileia* of the heavens. Indeed, the narrator presents Jesus undertaking prophetic tasks that call on divine power. Twice he feeds bread to multitudes with baskets of broken pieces left over

(14.13-21; 15.32-38) and, following the first of these feedings, he walks on water (14.22-27), a power generally associated with divine figures. These extraordinary accounts are, however, intimately linked to Jesus continuing to heal (14.34-36; 15.29-31); together, they call forth proclamations of faith: the disciples who encounter Jesus walking on the water proclaim him as 'Son of God' (14.33), the woman called Canaanite calls forth healing from him as *Kyrios* ('Lord') and 'Son of David' (15.22, 25, 27), while the crowds who see his healings glorify 'the God of Israel' (15.31), and Peter names him *Christos* and 'Son of the living God' at Caesarea Philippi (16.16).

This Jesus, who proclaims the *basileia* of the heavens and heals many who are plagued by illness, is seen to share in the power of God and is named in intimate relationship with God: God is with God's people and with their world/the Earth, the Emmanuel text of 1.23 professes. The Matthean narrator strains to understand this extraordinary divine/human relationship and to name Jesus in accordance with it. Much scholarship has been undertaken to seek to understand such titles as they might have functioned for the first-century Matthean community. This section (13.53–17.27) is certainly a turning point in the Matthean narrative for both disciples and opponents of Jesus as he looks toward Jerusalem, the place where he knows that he will suffer (16.21 and 17.22-23).

Mission Continues en Route to and within the City of Jerusalem

En route to Jerusalem and even within the city itself, Jesus' work continues. Matthew 18 has been designated the 'community discourse' as the narrator lays out the community's response to a member who becomes lost (18.10-14) and members who give offense to one another (18.15-20, 21-35). Forgiveness and restoration of right relationships are at the core of this discourse. For a community holding that in Jesus God is present among them (1.23) and that the raised Jesus continues to be present (28.20), a key verse is this: 'where two or three are gathered together in my name, there am I in the midst of them' (18.20). As the Shekinah is present when two or more sit down to study the Torah together, so too does Jesus' presence remain among his community when they gather in his name.

With the journey continuing (Mt. 19.1-2), the narrative presents Jesus also continuing his ministry of healing (19.2; 20.29-34; 21.14) and teaching but the opposition continues to mount (19.3). The narrator gathers diverse teachings in this narrative section (Matthew 19–23)—on divorce (19.3-9), discipleship (19.16-22; 20.20-28), resurrection (22.23-33) and in parables (20.1-16; 21.28-32, 33-45; 22.1-14). And the storyline advances: Jesus enters into the city to the cry of the crowds—'Hosanna to the Son of David… This is the prophet Jesus from Nazareth of Galilee' (21.1-11). The people's cry echoes back across the narrative to the opening words of the Gospel and the infancy narrative (1.1) and to the close of that infancy narrative (2.23)—'Jesus, Son of David…from Nazareth in the district of Galilee'. It is this prophet who takes on the prophetic act of clearing commerce out of the temple in words and actions reminiscent of Jeremiah 7 and then teaching in the temple precincts. It is not surprising that further opposition mounts (22.15, 34).

The most difficult segment of the Matthean narrative is what is often called Jesus' diatribe against the scribes and Pharisees (Matthew 23). It is on this that scholarly arguments rest as to whether the Matthean community was still within Judaism or if they had severed ties with the synagogue. Given the severity of the critique from the perspective of twenty-first century sensibilities and codes of speech, one is tempted to imagine that the break must have definitely occurred. As we will observe in a later chapter, social-scientific approaches to the Gospel have, however, provided us in recent decades with models to understand this diatribe. The teaching/preaching role of the scribes and Pharisees is affirmed by Jesus in the opening verses (23.1-3), as similar teaching/preaching roles are being legitimated in the community among those who believe that Jesus is the authorized teacher of the law. It is the way those roles are exercised by the scribes and Pharisees which is so severely critiqued by Matthew's Jesus and the language throws down a challenge to the segment of the community who have not accepted Jesus as their teacher. By way of this discourse, the role of the community's teachers and preachers who accept Jesus as the one who teaches what is of God is enhanced over against that segment of the community that identifies with the scribes and Pharisees. Community issues continue to shape Matthew's particular storytelling. Contemporary readers, however, need to beware of interpreting condemnations as historically descriptive.

The final discourse (Matthew 24–25) is often called the eschatological or apocalyptic discourse as it contains elements of those two worldviews that were current in first-century Judaism. While the discourse looks to an imaginary future (24.15-28, 29-31, 36-44), its emphasis is on how this circles back around to the present and makes ethical demands: watch (24.42; 25.13), be like the faithful and wise servant (24.45-51) or the good and faithful servant (25.14-30). This ethical proclamation reaches its climax in the very last teaching of Jesus, the parabolic judging of the nations by the Human One coming in glory. Whatever one does for the least (the hungry and thirsty, the stranger, the sick, and the imprisoned), this one proclaims as being done to him (Mt. 25.31-46, note especially 25.40). This is the climax of the ethic proclaimed by Jesus the preacher, teacher and healer, the proclaimer of the *basileia* of the heavens that is at hand.

Final Days

As we have noted, the Infancy Narrative provides an introductory frame for the five parallel narrative and discourse segments, so the final chapters (Matthew 26–28) form the other part of that frame as the Gospel narrative draws to a close. These chapters recount Jesus' condemnation and death and his being raised on the first day of the week following his crucifixion. While there are many similarities in the passion/resurrection narratives across the four Gospels, each is also a unique climax to the Gospel story that the particular evangelist has told.

Matthew's passion/resurrection narrative is framed by three thematics. The first is Jesus' relationship with the disciples. At the beginning he warns them yet again that he will be delivered up to be crucified (26.1-2); at the end of the narrative, he is reunited with them in Galilee and commissions them to teach all that he has taught—namely, the gospel (28.16-20). The second thematic framing the passion/resurrection narrative is controversy with the religious leaders. Initially the chief priests and elders determine to arrest and kill Jesus (26.3-5); at the end of the narrative, they continue to plot, concocting a story that will counter the guards' experience of the empty tomb (28.11-15). The third thematic is that of the women. In 26.6-13 we hear the story of the woman who pours healing ointment over the head of Jesus as he reclines at supper, recognizing and responding to his need for the healing that the ointment brings as he faces the death that he is sure will come. As Jesus has healed others, she now continues that healing role, this time for Jesus himself. Similarly at the end of the narrative, we see women (Mary Magdalene, Mary the mother of James and Joseph and the mother of the sons of Zebedee) who function as faithful disciples, waiting with the crucified one at the cross (27.55-56), watching at the grave (27.61: the two Marys), and going to see the tomb on the first day of the week (28.1-10: again, the two Marys). Disciples, opponents and a small group of women characterize the relationship with and responses to Jesus through this dramatic narrative as they have through the unfolding story; their characterization reaches a climax here.

The disciples all flee following the arrest of Jesus in the garden (26.56) with only Peter and Judas making subsequent appearances: Peter denies knowing anything of Jesus (26.69-75), and Judas, who repents of his betrayal of Jesus, goes out and hangs himself when the high priests and elders refuse to take back the 30 pieces of silver (27.3-10). Throughout the narrative the explicitly named 'disciples', either as a group or as individuals, fluctuate between understanding Jesus' *basileia* proclamation and not understanding, between demonstrating faith and having little faith. This climaxes in their abandonment of their teacher and leader in his time of need. In contrast to the disciples of John who take away his body and bury it as is characteristic of disciples (14.12), those of Jesus are conspicuously absent until the angel at the tomb summons them, through the agency of the two Marys, to go to Galilee from where Jesus re-commissions them to go out to teach, as he had, the message of the *basileia* of the heavens (28.16-20).

The religious leaders function as a dominant character group in the passion of Jesus. The 'chief priests and elders' (i.e. the Jerusalem authorities) send out those who arrest Jesus (26.47) and they bring him to the high priest, Caiaphas, and before the Sanhedrin, where he is questioned by the high priest and charged with blasphemy (26.57-68). They, in turn, hand Jesus over to the Roman governor, Pilate, who, despite the warnings received by his wife in a dream that Jesus is a righteous one (note this emphasis that has characterized Jesus' teaching) rather than a brigand, condemns Jesus to death at the urgings of the people persuaded by the chief priests and elders (27.15-23). The narrating of Pilate's washing of his hands of the blood of Jesus (27.24-26) further emphasizes the Matthean Gospel's laying of responsibility for the death of Jesus in the hands of the religious leaders, especially the Jerusalem cohort, a theme that may well be indicative of the tensive relationships within this early Jewish Christian community rather than an historical memory or reality. Indeed the leaders ('chief priests with scribes and elders') are not content with the condemnation of Jesus; they join the Roman soldiers in mocking Jesus, evoking two key characterizations of Jesus in the unfolding Gospel story: the Saving One and Son of God (27.41-44). With an ultimate ironic twist, an irony which characterizes Matthew's passion/resurrection narrative as a whole, the 'chief priests and the Pharisees' request of Pilate that they might set up a guard at the tomb of Jesus because they want to foil any attempts by Jesus' disciples to claim that he has been raised. It is a foil that is doubly ironic: Jesus' disciples have fled, as the reader has been told, and hence are not going to be involved in a heist such as the leaders fear; and with no intervention on the part of these disciples, Jesus is proclaimed raised from the dead by an angel who speaks to the women at the empty tomb (28.2-6). Clearly the theme of opposition to Jesus attributed to the Jewish leaders as a developing thread in the Matthean narrative reaches an ironic highpoint in the passion narrative in a way that is indicative of a growing tension around leadership in the community. The height of that irony is the framing narrative of 28.11-15, where the leaders are plotting to control the narrative of Jesus' resurrection.

In the third thematic that frames Matthew's account of the passion and resurrection of Jesus, the women are characterized by fidelity. Nowhere in the Gospel is such praise given to the action of a faithful follower of Jesus as that of the unnamed woman who pours out healing *myron* ('ointment') over the head of Jesus as he reclines at the first of his 'last suppers' (26.6-13). Jesus says of her action that it is a good deed done 'to me' just as the actions done for the hungry, the thirsty, the stranger and the sick would be done 'to me' he proclaims in the last great parable (25.40). It is this action—'what she has done'—that is to be remembered wherever the gospel is preached. This is the climax of discipleship in the unfolding narrative and it is represented by the action of this unnamed woman. Such a climax is augmented by the second half of the frame in which three narratives coalesce. Many women stand at the place of crucifixion having 'followed' Jesus from Galilee (a term indicative of discipleship in 4.20, 22, 25; 8.1, 22; 9.9; 10.38; 16.24; 19.21, 27-28; 20.34) and they are characterized as doing *diakonia* ('service') in relation to Jesus who has earlier characterized his own ministry as doing such *diakonia* (20.28). Two of these women watch faithfully at the tomb (27.61) and their witness continues to the dawn of the Sabbath when they go to observe or see the tomb and discover the stone has been rolled back (28.1-2). A heavenly messenger commissions these faithful women to go and proclaim to the disciples who have fled that Jesus has indeed been raised. But not only that, the risen one who is simply named finally meets them (28.9-10) and commissions them to tell the disciples to go to Galilee where they will be reconciled with Jesus.

These women represent faithful discipleship and their presence in the narrative of Jesus' passion/resurrection is highly significant. They have not only been faithful to the very foot of the cross of Jesus but have been commissioned as the first to proclaim the resurrection. Only three other minor female characters appear in the narrative: the two maids who challenge Peter to claim his discipleship and the wife of Pilate who receives a dream as Joseph did in the infancy narrative—a dream that could have prevented Jesus' death. None, however, is able to change the relentless course of the narrative once it is in play in the hands of the Jewish and Roman authorities. In the face of this wave of power, however, the fidelity of women at the beginning and end of the narrative is highly significant.

Within these three frames the narrative of Jesus' death unfolds. He faithfully celebrates a second 'last supper' with his disciples, this one being a Passover meal and in this context he offers broken bread and pours out wine to his disciples as an invitation into his own passion. In the Gospel of Matthew, however, Jesus does not invite his disciples to repeat this meal in his memory; instead, this meal indicates that he shall not participate in it until the time of fulfillment—the *basileia* of God. He prays in the garden for the strength to face what lies ahead if it cannot be taken away and then moves almost silently into his condemnation and death. We hear few words (26.64; 27.11) except the loud cry from the cross: 'My God, my God, why have you forsaken me?' (27.46). This prayer of the suffering just psalmist Jesus makes his own before he breathes his last. The one birthed to be savior (1.22), the one confirmed in his ministry to proclaim the *basileia* of the heavens by his baptism (3.13-17) through preaching, teaching and healing (4.23; 9.35), this one has suffered a most ignominious death at the hands of the Roman imperial system. He has been profoundly dishonoured.

The Gospel narrative does not end there with the death of this prophetic figure who stands within the line of Israel's prophets. By way of an empty tomb narrative, the evangelist proclaims that Jesus who had been crucified has been raised (28.5-6). This is augmented with two appearance stories: one to the women commissioned to tell Jesus' brothers to go to Galilee; and one to the eleven disciples who are commissioned to continue the work of Jesus (i.e. making disciples, baptizing and teaching). The Matthean evangelist claims at the beginning of the Gospel that God is with us, the Earth community, in the Jesus who was born of a woman (1.23). This same evangelist closes the narrative with the proclamation of the Jesus crucified and raised from entombment within the earth that he would continue with the entire Earth community to the end of the age (28.20).

Chapter 2

Reading the Matthean Narrative with Recent Scholars

I am with you always
to the end of the age (Mt. 28.20).

While the promise of the Matthean Jesus is to be with the community of believers 'to the end of the age', there is not the same continuity in Matthean scholarship either of people or of approaches. Indeed, as we prepared this Guide, we learnt of the deaths of Professor R.T. France, a long-standing colleague in Matthean studies, and of Professor Jane Schaberg, a scholar of Matthew's Infancy Narrative. There may, indeed, have also been others. We wish to honour their significant contributions to the study of the Gospel of Matthew as well as that of those scholars who have newly joined the ranks of Matthean studies. Also, in the period under consideration—mid 1990s to the present—there has been a consolidation of new approaches that emerged in the 1980s: literary critical approaches (such as narrative, reader-response, and audience oriented criticisms), the social-scientific approach and the socio-rhetorical methodology (which combines literary and social-scientific approaches in a nuanced way). This consolidation of methodologies has been accompanied by developing reader-oriented perspectives: feminist, masculinity, queer, postcolonial, indigenous and ecological, to name the major trends. And while many scholars have returned to the questions of the previous decades—sources, settings, structure, use of the Old Testament and the Law—some have moved Matthean scholarship in new directions as well as returning to well-worked themes, especially Christology and ecclesiology. This scholarship has found expression in new commentaries, in monographs and in collections of articles.

The newcomer to Matthean scholarship would do well to consult Mark Allan Powell's edited collection, *Methods for Matthew* (2009), to gain an overview of the three major methodological fields in contemporary biblical studies and the way these have functioned and continue to function in Matthean studies: historical-critical (in which the key concern is discerning the meaning intended by the original author of the text), new literary (whose focus is on the text and reader in the discerning of meaning), and social-scientific (which engages with contemporary social-scientific theories to determine historical meaning).

These methodologies are frameworks informed by particular philosophical positions in relation to the location and process of meaning making (e.g. whether meaning resides predominantly with author, text or reader). In this sense they are informed by a worldview in relation to meaning making. They are also accompanied by tools for analyzing the text, sets of questions and tasks to be undertaken. And so, for instance, redaction critics study parallel texts of the Synoptic Gospels, narrative critics focus on character, settings and rhetorical techniques, while reader-response criticism gives attention to the focalizing power of the text in shaping the reader's meaning-making activity. Each of these methodologies is accessed by scholars in a variety of ways and hence they will always be nuanced in a particular study. We will highlight some of these nuances in approach across the last decade and a half of Matthean studies.

In this Guide, we seek to make a distinction between a scholar's choice of a methodology or methodologies and the particular perspective or interpretive lens that each one brings to the text. The technical term for such an interpretive lens is a 'hermeneutic'. Within Powell's *Methods for Matthew*, you will find two essays on specific hermeneutical approaches: feminist and postcolonial. Those employing one of these or of a number of other hermeneutics that we will address also make use of one or other of the major methodologies. And so you will find feminist literary critical studies (see Cheyne 1996), masculinity social-scientific approaches (see Neyrey 2003) and ecological, socio-rhetorical readings (see Chapter 5). As far as possible, we will draw attention to a scholar's choice of methodology and hermeneutic and how these function to make meaning of the Matthean text. Unfortunately, not all scholars make their hermeneutic explicit but it is often revealed as their study unfolds.

As you read this chapter, you are invited to meet and engage with some recent scholars of the Gospel of Matthew whose work has emerged as book-length commentaries on the Gospel, or special studies that take up a particular theme or aspect of the Gospel text. In subsequent chapters, some additional approaches to the Gospel that are not included here will be discussed in more depth.

Historical-Critical Approaches and Commentaries

The publication of the three-volume work by Dale C. Allison and W.D. Davies beginning almost three decades ago (1988; 1991; 1997) could be regarded as the pinnacle of historical-critical exegesis of the Gospel of Matthew. Despite its exhaustive discussion of the structure, sources and composition of the text—all key elements of the historical-critical approach—scholars continue to find new things to say about the possible historical and socio-religious context of the author/s of the Gospel.

Historical criticism, as an umbrella term, covers a range of methodologies that seek to discover aspects of the world behind the Gospel text. What literary sources from the 'world behind the text' have been incorporated into this Gospel story? How have such sources been edited to produce a new perspective on the story of Jesus? What can we know about the community that produced this text? How might the text address concerns in the first-century Matthean community? And what, if any, aspects of the historical Jesus, as distinct from the Jesus of the text, are encoded within the Gospel story?

Biblical commentaries generally consist of an introductory and background section, in which scholars situate the Matthean community who produced the Gospel and the likely date of its composition, followed by detailed exegesis of the biblical text itself. As you read recent commentaries, note that there is, unfortunately, a tendency within some historical-critical scholarship to downplay or even mask the importance of hermeneutical factors shaping the reading experience by assuming a 'value neutral' outlook of *reasonable objectivity*. Historical-critical and hermeneutical approaches need not become dichotomized, however, as some contributions to Matthean scholarship, especially those explored in subsequent chapters, will explicitly take up and name the reader-oriented aspect of their approach while also working carefully with the socio-historical and cultural context of the text itself.

In engaging recent Matthean scholars, it becomes apparent that most scholars of Matthew today still hold to the two-source theory behind the composition of the Matthew. Readers of the canonical Gospels have long seen a connection between Matthew, Mark and Luke, leading them to be classified as 'Synoptic' because they can be seen together (in Greek, *opsis* means 'seen' and *sun* means 'together/with'). This hypothesis posits that the author of the Gospel of Matthew used a number of literary sources in the compilation of the Gospel. These sources include the Gospel of Mark as well as the hypothetical source 'Q' (from *Quelle*, which means 'source' in German), which contains material shared also by the author of Luke but not by Mark. The Gospel of Matthew also contains special material unique to this Gospel and not contained in the other Synoptic Gospels; the source for such unique material is labeled 'M'. These theories about sources underpin redaction criticism, which seeks to explicate how the Matthean redactor used the various sources available.

While most scholars still assume Markan priority, there has been a notable shift among a minority of recent scholars to an earlier dating of the Gospel. A previous generation typically dated the composition of Matthew to the 80s or 90s of the first century CE. This dating supposed that the Gospel of Mark, which Matthew engaged as a source, was written around or slightly before the time of the destruction of the Jewish temple in 70 CE.

Recent arguments for an earlier dating for Mark's gospel have led Craig Evans (2012), R.T. France (2007) and John Nolland (2005) to opt for an earlier date for the composition of Matthew around or before 70 CE. Other scholars are less favourable to this reassessment, however, and cautiously settle for the customary date around the 80s or 90s CE.

Finally, while most commentators still regard the individual author of the Gospel of Matthew as an anonymous Jewish Christian, a minority of scholars have more recently stated their preference for attributing such authorship to Matthew the tax-collector (Mt. 9.9), the traditional author designated by the early church beginning (as far as we know) a century after its initial composition. Evans (2012), France (2007) and Keener (2009) all describe Matthew as a 'possible' or 'likely candidate' for the authorship of the Gospel, although none attempt to establish this position beyond conjecture. Such arguments regarding the authorship of Matthew usually have as their point of departure a single piece of external evidence attributed to Papias, which contains the earliest attribution to the apostle Matthew. Papias' attribution is preserved in Eusebuis, *Historia ecclesiastica*, 3.39: 'Matthew, then, compiled the oracles in the Hebrew/Aramaic language, and each interpreted/translated them as they were able'. The Gospel text itself gives nothing away as to the naming of its author. One could argue, however, that the call of Matthew the disciple in Mt. 9.9 would seem to discount Matthean authorship as one would expect a more first-hand, eyewitness account if the disciple was the author rather than a formula call narrative which has already been used in Mt. 4.18-22.

As you begin to read scholarly commentaries along with your own reading of the Matthean text, you might consult the following recent ones that utilize the historical-critical approach. John Nolland's *The Gospel of Matthew* (2005) is, broadly speaking, redaction-critical; focusing on the Greek text of the Gospel, its technical discussion of the Greek text is most useful. R.T. France's commentary, *The Gospel of Matthew* (2007), might be considered somewhat more of a 'fresh' reading. Drawing on his vast experience as a Matthean scholar, France does not worry too much about locating himself within constantly moving academic debates. Indeed, he claims to have written the first draft of his commentary on each pericope of Matthew before looking at any other commentaries (including even his own earlier one). France provides a lively English translation at the beginning of each section, using contemporary idioms and giving priority to 'clarity over literary elegance' (France 2007: xix). He then places the text in its historical context and considers common narrative and redactional issues, but does not develop in detail a strict method and/or hermeneutic. What does come across, however, is his appreciation for the Gospel's characterization of Jesus as the fulfillment of Jewish messianic expectations, as well as its theological exposition of ethical life in the kingdom of heaven.

In his commentary on the beatitudes (Mt. 5.1-12), for instance, France observes how the Matthean text shifts the sayings in a spiritual direction (e.g. 'Blessed are the poor *in spirit*', 5.3), and promotes an idealized form of the 'good life' in the kingdom (2007: 158). This contrasts with the Lucan beatitudes (Lk. 6.20-26) that speak more of the disciples' own material woes and social disadvantage in their efforts to follow Jesus.

If you encounter Craig S. Keener's two lengthy commentaries you could be forgiven for thinking that he wrote the same book twice. Keener's 2009 *The Gospel of Matthew: A Socio-Rhetorical Commentary* is, in fact, almost identical to his earlier book, *A Commentary on the Gospel of Matthew* (1999), except for an addendum on Matthew and Greco-Roman rhetoric (Keener 2009: xxv-xlix). Keener's methodological approach has more in common with traditional historical-critical scholarship (using source, form and redaction criticisms, as well as 'hard data' from archeological and literary sources) than with more recent socio-rhetorical developments that incorporate both the work of social-scientific biblical criticism as well as ideological, hermeneutical and reader-oriented perspectives.

A recent commentary is that of Craig A. Evans's *Matthew* (2012), which appears in the *New Cambridge Bible Commentary* series. He explores the Matthean text's historical, social and religious context in the first century. For Evans, Jesus is best understood within his Jewish background and context, and he believes that the Gospel offers a somewhat reliable portrayal of the life of Jesus. The author of Matthew wrote his Gospel in a time of transition when he and his first readers, most of whom were Jewish Christians, had been driven out of the synagogue and were beginning to form a new community outside of the traditional structures of late first-century Judaism. Evans' commentary is useful for its references to related texts, both internal and external to the biblical canon; these references shed light on the meaning of Matthew's use of words, phrases and concepts within his first-century historical context. He applies his vast knowledge of early Jewish, Rabbinic and Greco-Roman literature to understanding Matthew's portrayal of Jesus' life and teaching.

Finally, we draw attention to Warren Carter's *Matthew and the Margins: A Socio-Political and Religious Reading* (2000), which is especially distinctive among the selection of commentaries mentioned above. Carter reads the Gospel by emphasizing the roles that marginality and Roman imperial power play in shaping the Matthean community behind the text. He contends that Matthew's Gospel functions first and foremost as a 'counternarrative' in its rejection of Rome and imperial rule: it is situated on the margins of and in opposition to the dominant Roman imperial culture and society. Through a close reading of the text employing an explicit hermeneutic of 'marginality', Carter demonstrates how Matthew's Gospel negotiates and legitimates a *marginal* identity for the community of disciples around Jesus (at the same time identifying his own experience as a marginal immigrant to the United States). One example of his hermeneutic of marginality is evident in his discussion of the beatitudes. He contends that they express the literal deprivation of God's people and, in particular, the terrible consequences of Roman imperial power (note that this is the exact opposite of France's observation that Matthew casts them as 'spiritual woes'). The impact of 'empire studies' on Matthean scholarship in recent years, as demonstrated in Carter's commentary, will be taken up at greater length in the next chapter.

Emerging Literary Approaches and the Study of Matthew

Text-oriented and narrative critics analyze texts synchronically, focusing on two aspects of the narrative: story and discourse. Story is the narrative interrelationship of settings, events and characters that constitute the plot. Discourse includes the rhetorical devices that function to shape the narrative: repetitions, irony, parallelism and framing to name but a few. As scholars develop and utilize this approach, they have combined a range of aspects of the methodology for their reading of the Matthean text.

Narrative critics have not, however, embraced the genre of commentary as historical critics have for decades. Indeed the Abingdon series, *Interpreting Biblical Texts*, is almost unique in taking up this approach in commentary form. It provides a place for scholars to addresses critical issues within the Gospel text, and explore the world created by the text in the process of contemporary readerly engagement rather than in terms of its historical audience. Donald Senior writes the Matthew Commentary in this series and he is concerned primarily with the 'textual world' of Matthew's Gospel, using its categories of plot, setting and characterization to determine the meaning evoked for the reader. For Senior, the beatitudes in Mt. 5.3-16 alert the reader to the scope of Matthew's theological vision. He also highlights the eschatological perspective of the beatitudes, that is, their concern with the end of time, the Day of Judgment and the final destination of humankind. Senior argues that this perspective becomes a foundation for the ethical teaching within the developing Gospel narrative. Acts of mercy, reconciliation and peacemaking are in accord with the intent of God and the true nature of the human person, thus one can anticipate the reality of the kingdom of heaven now and live ethically in the fullness of God's reign.

A range of narrative approaches has, however, characterized recent monographs in which scholars explore particular Gospel themes. Below we will demonstrate not only the scholarly approach to interpretation but also some of the key emphases.

Clearly at the heart of the Gospel of Matthew is its characterization of Jesus and readers will have noted that the opening verse of the Gospel identifies this Jesus as *Christos* or Messiah (Mt. 1.1). That this naming functions as a literary thematic is evident as the reader traces its sixteen uses across the narrative from 1.1–27.22. Jason Hood explores this thematic in *The Messiah, His Brothers, and the Nations* (2011). He examines the phrases 'Judah and his brothers' and 'Judah and Jeconiah and his brothers' (1.2, 11) as well as the inclusion of four women in Jesus' genealogy (1.2-6). For Hood, biblical genealogies carry a narrative function, connecting the story of Israel, as presented in the genealogy, to Jesus and his mission. On the one hand, because Judah and Jeconiah are sacrificial kings (Gen. 49.8-10; 2 Kgs 25.27-30; Jer. 52.31-34), both characters can be seen as forerunners of the Messiah. On the other hand, by mentioning four women, Matthew's Gospel, instead of accentuating their gender, emphasizes their Gentile origin. Hence Hood argues that by including these women, Matthew's story shows Gentile nations may become righteous and faithful by submitting their loyalty to Judah's royal son, who is identified as *Christos*/ Messiah.

As the Matthean Gospel unfolds, the meaning of the designation *Christos* is made clearer to the readers. In Mt. 11.2-6, Jesus answers John's question as to whether he is the awaited *Christos*/Messiah with these words: 'the blind receive their sight, the lame walk, the lepers are cleansed, the deaf hear, the dead are raised, and the poor have good news brought to them' (11.5). The Messiah is a doer of deeds of righteousness in the Matthean narrative.

Alistair Wilson in *When will These Things Happen? A Study of Jesus as Judge in Matthew 21–25* (2004) explores an aspect of Jesus' messiahship that augments the political and social factors evident in 11.2-6. It is that aspect with which many contemporary readers are less comfortable, namely Jesus as a judge in many scenes from Matthew 21–25. For Wilson, however, Matthew 21–25 interweaves Jesus' social, political and religious judgment against religious leaders with his future prediction of the destruction of the temple. The approach he uses is that of composition criticism, which functions as a bridge between redaction criticism as a tool within historical criticism and the newer literary approaches. Composition criticism analyzes the text as a whole, determining what motivated the composition of the text and what compositional procedures the authors used. This approach functioned as a bridge to the more recent literary approaches.

The reader of the Matthean Gospel is aware from the very beginning of the narrative that Jesus is being characterized through the lens of the Jewish scriptures. This is evident in the opening verse, in the genealogy that follows, in the fulfillment citations that are particularly visible in Matthew 1–2 (1.22; 2.15, 17, 23) and at various other places throughout the narrative. The text of the prophet Isaiah provides a significant source for such intertexts. It is not surprising, therefore, that Richard Beaton would undertake his study,

Isaiah's Christ in Matthew's Gospel (2002). After asserting that some literary evidence regarding the use of Isa. 42.1-4 in a messianic and eschatological sense in the first-century could explain Matthew's use of the text, he claims that Isa. 42.1-4 is used at two different but complementary levels in Matthew: the narrative and the theological. At the narrative level, the quotations are used to validate what Jesus has done previously. In the case of Mt. 12.14-16, Isaiah's quotation is employed to validate and explain Jesus' withdrawal and Jesus' warning about not telling anyone who he was. At the theological level, Isaianic quotations are used to highlight Jesus' teachings and messianic perspective.

Joel Willitts's *Matthew's Messianic Shepherd-King: In Search of 'the Lost Sheep of the House of Israel'* (2007) explores the messianic motif from a different perspective: namely, that of shepherd-king. He locates this within the context of Davidic messianism and its first-century political ramifications. Using composition and audience-oriented criticism, Willitts affirms that in first-century Palestine the Davidic Messiah and Israel's Shepherd-king motifs were used as instruments of hope for a political-national restoration of Israel's kingdom, including the territorial restoration of the Land of Israel. Having this concept in mind, Willitts focuses on the phrase 'the lost sheep of the house of Israel', which is repeated twice in Matthew's Gospel (10.6; 15.24), and argues that the phrase is a reference to the remnants of the former Northern Kingdom of Israel who were still residing in Galilee and the northern regions of Israel. Accordingly, Jesus' mission in Matthew's Gospel is toward this limited geographic and ethnic group.

Study of the titles given to Jesus in the Matthean narrative can tend, however, to turn scholarly attention away from the mission of Jesus: his preaching, teaching and healing (see 4.23; 9.35). Evert-Jan Vledder's *Conflict in the Miracle Stories: A Socio-Exegetical Study of Mathew 8 and 9* (1997) remedies that a little. He locates the Matthean community in Galilee and Syria and proposes a mixed membership of not only Jews and Gentiles, but also of urban non-elite and rural peasantry, such as pariahs, the unclean and the expendable classes. According to Vledder, who employs a social-scientific methodology, Matthew 8 and 9 show that while the Matthean community and Jesus were on the side of the marginalized, the Jewish leaders were on the side of the Roman rulers and belonged to the retainer class of their society. So, whilst in Matthew 8 and 9 the Jewish leaders legitimize their own interest, Jesus and the Matthean community act on behalf of the interests of the marginalized. This provides a lens then through which readers can read other segments of the Matthean narrative and its construction of the mission of Jesus.

That mission characterizes the heart of the Matthean Gospel is evident in the programmatic text, Mt. 4.17: 'From that time Jesus began to proclaim, "Repent, for the kingdom of heaven has come near"'. Margaret Hannan in

The Nature and Demands of the Sovereign Rule of God in the Gospel of Matthew (2006), another significant contributor to the study of Matthew's Gospel who died during the course of our researching for this volume, turns an audience-oriented approach to a study of a central Matthean thematic that characterizes the ministry of Jesus—the kingdom of heaven—by analysing the term 'kingdom' and the phrase 'kingdom of heaven' in the Gospel of Matthew. Meticulously examining the thematic of the kingdom as a developing and unifying element of the narrative, she argues that it provides a theological perspective on the nature of God's sovereignty and presence—a call to transformation which will be accomplished as soon as men and women respond to God's call. In Hannan's view, God's call is an invitation to enter into covenant relationship with God in order to inaugurate a world shaped by compassion, freedom, equity and peace. The 'kingdom of heaven' does not, therefore, refer to a final end or a specific event, but to a worldwide change. It is this that characterizes Jesus programmatic proclamation not only in 4.17 but also as he enacts it with the unfolding of the narrative.

Jonathan Pennington in *Heaven and Earth in the Gospel of Matthew* (2007) also analyzes the phrase 'kingdom of heaven' in Matthew's Gospel. Unlike Mark and Luke who use the term 'kingdom of God' (e.g. Mk 1.15; Lk. 17.20-21), Matthew is the only one who uses the phrase 'kingdom of heaven' (e.g. Mt. 4.17). This difference has been commonly explained as a Matthean circumlocution for the name of God, assuming a Jewish background for Matthew's Gospel and hence an avoidance of speaking the divine name unnecessarily. This suggests that the 'kingdom of God' in Mark and Luke, and the 'kingdom of heaven' in Matthew are two ways of describing the same teaching, suggesting an identical meaning for both terms in the Synoptic Gospels. Pennington draws on his careful literary analysis to critique this assumption of Jewish circumlocution for God's name, especially in light of the Matthean use of the phrase 'kingdom of God' (12.28; 19.24; 21.31, 43) four times in the Gospel. Rather, he argues that in Matthew's Gospel, the phrase 'kingdom of heaven' is used to emphasize God's kingdom. According to Pennington, the phrase seeks to show that God's kingdom is not on earth but in heaven. It differs, therefore, from earthly kingdoms; indeed, its manifestation will be eschatological, implying that the 'kingdom of heaven' will replace these earthly kingdoms. The repeated use of 'heaven' and 'earth' as a pair in different phrases in the Gospel functions to describe the universality of God's dominion, and encourage the Matthean readers to see themselves as the true people of God. Choosing to be part of the kingdom that is in heaven, they are, indeed, in opposition to earthly Roman and Jewish rulers.

In the Gospel of Matthew, the proclamation of the kingdom/*basileia* of the heaven/s is not unique to Jesus. Indeed, it has already characterized the ministry of John the Baptist (3.2). Gary Yamasaki in *John the Baptist in Life and Death: Audience-Oriented Criticism of Matthew's Gospel* (1998) examines the role of John the Baptist in the Gospel of Matthew. He concludes that the character John makes little significant contribution at the story-level of the narrative. In fact, he claims that much of the narrative surrounding John could easily be deleted without causing any significant impact on the story. At the discourse level, however, Yamasaki asserts that John's role is extremely significant. John contributes critical insight into the positive characterization of Jesus and the negative characterization of the Jewish leaders, thus shaping the opinion of the reader. According to Yamasaki, the implied author uses the figure of John to affect the reader's perspective while reading Matthew's story. Although Yamasaki's title suggests an audience-oriented approach situating the text and readers in a particular socio-historical context, the work gives little attention to this.

Audience orientation does, however, characterize the work of Warren Carter and John Paul Heil in *Matthew's Parables: Audience-Oriented Perspectives* (1998). They describe a dynamic process between the text and the context in which Matthew's Gospel was produced, suggesting that in order to hear the Matthean parables as the Matthean audience would, interpreters need to take account of the audience's capacity to understand koine Greek and socio-historic elements such as king, centurion, leper or householder. Carter and Heil also seek to demonstrate that the audience understands the parables in terms of the narrative progression that characterizes texts. They argue that the Matthean audience would hear the Matthean parables as an invitation to discipleship in the context of the narrative.

Some Final Observations and Conclusion

This survey of a range of studies in Matthew's Gospel has not been exhaustive. It has rather drawn attention to the range of topics as well as approaches that should provide the newcomer to the study of the Gospel of Matthew with a wealth of scholarship for exploration and guidance. An analysis of the above suggests some interesting points to consider. First, in the past decade, there has been a growing interest in Matthean studies, with new focused studies appearing each year since 2002. Second, although it is true that the field of Matthean studies is mostly occupied by men, there have been significant contributions made by women. Third, though many studies, like the commentaries, focus mainly on historical-critical issues, there is an emergent tendency to examine the Matthean text using literary or eclectic lenses. Fourth, we see a small number of Matthean scholars coming from Oceania and Africa but the vast majority are still located in North America and Europe. Sadly, we could not find Latin American or Asian-based Matthean scholars writing or publishing in English.

In surveying some recent Matthean scholars and their approaches to interpreting the text, we have encountered the shifts in biblical scholarship to incorporate newer methodologies with the more traditional historical criticism. In conclusion, we will also note that some recent commentaries in particular are more explicitly theological and life-oriented than the ones we have introduced above. The primary objective for these commentaries is not so much a technical exploration of the history behind the text, but rather to apply and expound the Gospel for modern readers. Douglas R.A. Hare's 2009 commentary on Matthew in the *Interpretation* series, for example, fits into this category and is designed as an expository commentary to meet the needs of ministers and church readers. Similarly, Brendan Byrne's 2004 commentary, *Lifting the Burden: Reading Matthew's Gospel in the Church Today*, and Russell Pregeant's 2004 commentary on Matthew both take a theological-centered approach to the text. Finally, the 2003 commentary *The Gospel of Matthew: A Contextual Introduction for Group Study* by Daniel Patte, Monya A. Stubbs, Justin S. Ukpong and Revelation E. Velunta provides an introduction to the Gospel for Bible study groups in seminary and church settings. Hermeneutically speaking, these scholars are concerned primarily with the meaning of the text for Christian believers today, and less so with textual and historical matters, although these are intermittently discussed as the scholars deemed necessary.

As you continue your reading and your study of the Gospel of Matthew with the Gospel text in one hand and a scholarly work in the other, the next chapter will turn your attention to an area of Matthean scholarship that focuses a new type of attention on the Matthean context, namely its location within the Roman Empire and the implications of this location for interpreting the text.

Chapter 3

Reading the Matthean Narrative within Roman Imperialism

Repent for the Basileia of the heavens is near at hand (Mt. 3.2; 4.17).

While the previous chapter gave attention to trends in interpreting the text of Matthew's Gospel, we turn here to engagement with those studies that focus on determining the historical setting of the Gospel. Many scholars have argued for a Jewish community, probably located in Syrian Antioch. A current proponent of this view is David Sim (1998), who proposes a Jewish community of believers in Jesus as the source and recipients of the Matthean Gospel. They were not Christians, as we understand the term today, Sim suggests, but observers of the Jewish law who became followers of Jesus and the Jesus' story. He argues that the Matthean Gospel is not characterized by a mission to the Gentiles, and he explains the severe anti-Gentile tone as a result of Gentile persecution both during and after the Jewish war (66–73 CE).

In a similar vein, Michelle Slee (2003) strongly argues for the city of Antioch as the place where the Matthean community was located. In contrast to Sim, however, she focuses on the problem of Gentile entry into the church in Antioch, examining not only the Gospel of Matthew but also other documents such as the Books of Acts (Acts 15), Galatians (Gal. 2.1-14) and the *Didache*. Slee sees a difference between Matthew's Gospel and the *Didache* regarding the issue of Gentile Torah-observance. While in the Matthean community, the Gentiles were converted to Judaism and thus became Torah-observant, the Didachist allowed Gentiles to enter the community without taking on full Torah-observance. Slee explains these differences as an internal division within the Antioch community that was caused by the events described in Galatians 2, in which we can see a conflict regarding Torah-observance and Gentiles.

Anthony Saldarini (1994) also suggests a Jewish community context for the Gospel of Matthew. Unlike Sim and Slee, however, Saldarini does not ground his arguments only in historical exploration but also uses a social-scientific approach, particularly the sociological category of deviance. According to Saldarini, Matthew's Gospel addresses a deviant group within the Jewish community which seeks, albeit unsuccessfully, to reform it. In attempting to reach its goal, this sectarian Jewish group engages in polemics and harsh disputes with the Jewish community as a whole, showing a passionate interest in reforming its own people. One of the natural consequences of this argument is that it critiques the use of Matthew's Gospel as an anti-Jewish weapon, because, as Saldarini affirms, the Gospel of Matthew depicts Jews believing in Jesus, who show zeal for 'the lost sheep of the house of Israel' (Mt.10.6).

Although Aaron Gale (2005) claims something similar regarding the Jewishness of the Matthean Gospel, he differentiates himself from Sim, Slee and Saldarini by proposing Sepphoris, a prominent Galilean city just six kilometres north/north-west of Nazareth, as the place where the Matthean community was located. Although prior to Gale's work, J. Andrew Overman (1990) had proposed Galilee as a possible location of the Matthean community and suggested either Tiberias or Sepphoris, Gale is much more specific in his argument for Sepphoris. The members of the Matthean community, in Gale's view, were conservative Jewish Christians who not only remained loyal to the Torah but also were in conflict with an important Jewish community. Such a community, according to Gale, was likely located in Sepphoris, where a strong, bilingual and wealthy Jewish community can be traced textually and historically. Gale similarly argues that the members of the Matthean community were educated people with a traditional literacy level; this could explain, for Gale, the intricate techniques that we can see woven into the Matthean text, as well as its references to scribes and to the Torah.

The emphasis on Jewish culture and tradition evident in the Matthean Gospel is further explored by Anne O'Leary (2006), who investigates the use of Mark by Matthew as a literary source; such use by Matthew, in her opinion, was in accordance with the literary conventions of Greco-Roman antiquity. O'Leary therefore not only proposes a viable social setting, but also analyses the literary connections between ancient writings and Matthew's Gospel. By comparing different ancient texts, she asserts that it was common in the Greco-Roman world to re-write earlier texts by means of creative imitation. In the case of Matthew, she sees a strong dependence on Mark's Gospel; this suggests that the Matthean author creatively 'judaized' the Gospel of Mark, as seen, in particular, in Matthew's use of the Hebrew Bible and in the way that the Matthean author structures the Gospel by following a Jewish theological emphasis on numbers.

During this same period, without dismissing the case for Matthew's Jewish identity, several scholars propose an independent Jewish-Christian Matthean community. This entails a group of Jews and/or Gentiles who believed in Jesus but did not continue as participants of mainstream Judaism of the first century. This sectarian Jewish group, although separate, was constantly debating with the members of local Jewish synagogues about Torah issues while simultaneously establishing a distance between themselves and the Jewish community. While several scholars have advocated for such a position in the past, a current proponent of this position is Anthony Ewherido (2006). He argues that Matthew's Gospel presents and reflects such a division in Matthew 13, in which the Matthean Jesus employs parables to describe several kinds of separations. Ewherido focuses on the Gospel's distinction between members of the Jesus community who are represented by the disciples and the Jewish community, represented by non-disciples, that does not follow Jesus.

What becomes obvious from the ongoing attempts to reconstruct the Matthean community producing the Gospel and its location is that this Gospel does not stand alone but must be contextualized in a vibrant Jewish and emergent Christian and Graeco-Roman literary milieu. It is in such a context that the relationship between the Gospel of Matthew, the Didache and their constitutive communities of origin has emerged as a focal point in recent Matthean scholarship. It is commonly assumed that the Didache used the final form of Matthew's Gospel as a possible source and that the Didache, therefore, was written after Matthew's Gospel around the second century. These premises are, however, keenly debated. First, there is an emerging tendency among some scholars to assert that the Didache was written late in the first century. Representative of this tendency is Alan Garrow (2004). He suggests that the writer of the Gospel of Matthew is dependent on the Didache as a direct and main source. This, of course, involves assuming that the Didache was written before the Gospel of Matthew. However, a suggestion of this kind is problematic because such an early composition date for the Didache has not yet been established. However, if the Didache was written during the latter part of the first century, both documents may be related in their dependency on the same tradition, as André Tuilier (2005) argues. This suggests a similar and shared context for these two pieces of writing.

Either by assuming a Matthean dependence on the Didache, or vice versa, an analysis of Didache's social context has emerged as an important element for some scholars in establishing the social context of Matthew's Gospel. There are, however, different geographical and social settings that have been proposed for the Didache, such as Egypt, Palestine and Antioch, but none of them have found a strong scholarly consensus—a situation which parallels exploration of the socio-cultural and authorial context of the Gospel itself. One of the elements of context that can be argued with surety, however, is that the Gospel of Matthew was written against a backdrop of Roman imperialism.

Roman Imperialism and the Gospel of Matthew

Around the turn of the twenty-first century a new trend within New Testament studies in general and Matthean studies in particular began to emerge concerning the interface between Jesus, the early Christian movement and

Roman imperialism. Specifically, the question was raised: how has Roman imperialism, as the historical context surrounding the Gospel's production and early reception, impacted not only the shaping of the document but also some of its central themes and tenets? Previously, Matthean scholars had paid little attention to this dimension of the Gospel's world primarily because Rome is not explicitly mentioned within the text, and the emperor receives only a brief mention in 21.15-22. In more recent studies, the impact of Roman power on the early Jewish Christian movement has been understood as integral to the composition and early reception of the Gospel. Most of the scholars adopting such an approach would reject a common assumption present in many theological readings that Jesus and the Gospel writers were not interested in the political realities of their day.

The historical Jesus of Nazareth carried out his mission among an ancient Mediterranean people who were subjected to Roman imperial hegemony. The Matthean text was also composed in a time and place heavily dominated by Roman imperial influence that would likely have exerted itself over almost every sphere of peasant life. Such conditions were especially difficult for those living on the margins of the empire, both geographically and socially. If we locate the community that composed the Gospel of Matthew in either Antioch or Sepphoris, as has been argued by recent scholars and demonstrated above, we are aware that both these cities were considered significant Roman cities in the Syro-Palestinian region of the first century. Antioch was an important military and administrative centre for the empire, and was noted for the role it played in the defence of the empire's eastern borders. Warren Carter describes how Roman presence and imperial ideology were pervasive in the city and functioned as a constant reminder of Roman sovereignty over the people within its territories. This new stream of scholarship seeks to explore what effects Roman imperialism might have had on the Matthean community and its rendition of the story of Jesus, and how this can help us to better interpret the message of Matthews' Gospel.

A combination of methodologies have been employed by scholars to determine how Matthew's Gospel might demonstrate resistance to and/or negotiation with the Roman Empire's claims to sovereignty over the world through not only its social and political prescriptions but also its theological assertions. The section below begins with a survey of the Roman imperial background to the Gospel before exploring how a variety of directions using a combination of tools, from disciplines including the social sciences, empire studies and postcolonial theory, have been employed in recent Matthean scholarship.

The Meaning of Empire

The terms 'empire' and 'imperialism' can be used in both historical and political contexts. The word 'empire' typically describes a system of government in which a group of nations or peoples are ruled by a powerful sovereign or government. 'Imperialism' refers to the practice of extending the rule or authority of an empire; in other words, it denotes the behaviour of empires. Modern empire theorists tend to emphasize the behaviour of empires as a particular form of domination or control between two agents set apart by an unequal relationship. Such definitions emphasize a hierarchical structure or system in which an authority at or near the top dominates and controls those below.

The Roman Empire functioned as both a political ideology in the sense of Rome's belief in its right to command territories/peoples as sanctioned by the gods, and in a concrete geographical sense to refer to the area or land that was considered first and foremost Roman territory. At its height, this extended from Britain across most of Europe, through to the Middle East and along North Africa.

Roman society was based on an agrarian system of production and social ordering in which its wealth and power were grounded primarily in land. The rulers of the Empire were those who owned land and so could accumulate wealth off the back of cheap labour and high taxation on the production, distribution and consumption of goods. The means by which Rome was able to claim sovereignty over its territories was principally through coercion, given the might of its extensive military. Moreover, various forms of propaganda, including statues depicting the emperor and important events or figures in Roman history as well as the use of the emperor's face on coins, functioned to normalize and maintain Roman occupation in much the same way as dominant political ideologies exert themselves as the status quo today.

The Roman Empire's way of life was predominantly sustained by taxation. This enabled the ruling minority to acquire vast wealth that in turn supported the lifestyles of the wealthy and the funding of the imperial military and vast building projects. Taxation was heavy and disproportionately targeted the poor. Rome regarded the avoidance of tax payments as rebellion against Rome's sovereignty. Taxes were used to collect a 'surplus' from peasant production to support the elite way of life.

Matthew as a Counter-Narrative?

An emphasis on the Roman imperial context surrounding Matthew's Gospel was first navigated in a major way by Warren Carter beginning with his commentary *Matthew and the Margins: A Sociopolitical and Religious Reading*, which appeared in 2000 (and was briefly discussed in a previous chapter). While a number of possible responses to imperial rule appear within the Matthean text, Carter contends that Matthew's Gospel functions primarily as a 'counternarrative' in its rejection of Rome and imperial rule. It is, therefore, situated on the margins of and in opposition to the dominant Roman imperial culture and society. By counternarrative, Carter means a work of resistance that rejects explicit characteristics of the dominant culture and rhetoric to which it responds. In this sense, it functions to strengthen the Matthean communal identity and lifestyle as an alternative community. A counternarrative also evokes the creation of a more just society through voluntary reform by the dominant society in accordance with the vision of an alternative, better way of life.

Through his close reading of the text, Carter attempts to demonstrate how Matthew's Gospel negotiates and legitimates a marginal identity for the community of disciples. Important for Carter's thesis is his locating of the Matthean community as a small group of Christian disciples coming from a cross-section of society socioeconomically and living in the city of Antioch around the 80s CE. Building on the work of previous scholars he contends that the Gospel's audience is in tension with not only other members of the city's Jewish community, but also the values, commitments and agendas of the Roman Empire.

For Carter, a conflict between the margins, primarily represented by Jesus together with the disciples, and the centre, comprising the religious and political elite, forms the basis of the narrative of Matthew. The Gospel's point of view exposes and reacts against this centre negatively as a world that is oppressive, hierarchical and life-destroying. The audience are accordingly encouraged to form a commitment to the Gospel's advocating of certain perspectives, structures and practices associated with Jesus and God, and to faithfully reject those associated with the religious and political leaders who are aligned with Satan.

Carter continued to develop these insights with his 2001 book *Matthew and Empire*. In this book he assesses a number of texts in respect of their function as counternarratives: Mt. 1.21, which names Jesus as Saviour; 11.28-30, which invites readers to take up 'my yoke' and not Rome's; 17.24-27 in relation to paying taxes; and 27.11-26 at the heart of the Roman trial. Carter provides a detailed overview of the Roman imperial system, including its theological underpinnings and relationship to the Matthean community within Antioch. The book is also helpful in its survey of the 'networks of power' that operated and affected the social structures of the ancient Mediterranean. In surmising the impact of Roman imperialism on the everyday population in Syria and Palestine, Carter argues that Rome's presence also extends to theological claims made by the Roman system that ultimately came into conflict with those made in relation to Jesus. The emperor is presented as chosen by the gods to rule over the earth and is believed to be the agent of the gods' sovereignty—a claim similar to that which the emerging Jewish-Christian community was making for Jesus.

The Roman imperial system has been summarized thus across Carter's work:

- Basic to Roman imperial theology was the assertion that Rome rules because the gods have willed it. The gods were thought to be in control of history. Therefore, to go against Rome was to go against the gods.
- The emperor (*basileus*) is Jupiter's agent on Earth.
- The imagery of 'light' commonly denotes the emperor's presence.
- The Greek term *basileia*, which is usually translated into English as 'kingdom', is often used to refer to empires like Rome.

This leads Carter to develop a uniquely counter-imperial view of Matthean Christology. What specifically about Jesus and God did Matthew want to express to his readers? Traditional approaches to Matthean Christology have tended to focus on how titles attributed to Jesus primarily reflect certain beliefs about the divinity and humanity of Jesus. Additionally, many scholars have identified typological allusions between Jesus and various Old Testament figures, the most prominent example being Moses. Carter's exploration of Matthean Christology in Roman imperial purview does not necessarily come into conflict with these approaches, but certainly adds an important dimension to their historical understanding. The language of lordship/*kyrios*, kingdom/*basileia* and so on, functions as antilanguage in its subversion of the Roman imperial norm.

Carter observes the remarkable (but typically unnoticed) similarity between claims made by Roman imperial theology about the emperor and empire and the Matthean presentation of Jesus as God's salvific agent. He argues that this functions to contest the assertion that the emperor represents the gods' sovereignty, will and divine blessing on earth by presenting Jesus as a theological and social challenge to the empire. The Gospel presents an alternative understanding of the world in presenting Jesus' subversion of imperial claims.

Richard A. Horsley has also given considerable attention to developing readings of the New Testament as counter-imperial literature. In relation to Matthew's Gospel in particular, he analyses the nativity narratives in Matthew 1–2 and Luke 1–3 from the heightened backdrop of the political situation of first-century Palestine. He argues that traditional interpretations of the infancy narratives, within both the church and academy, have domesticated these texts in ways that have meant losing their counter-cultural edge.

Recognition that the infancy narratives have little if any historical basis has led to an intense focus on the theology of the text by scholars. For example, the repeated emphasis on geographical names and prophecy fulfilment citations within the flight to Egypt (Mt. 2.13-23) are often seen to primarily serve an apologetic purpose: how did Jesus the messiah come from Nazareth in Galilee and not from Bethlehem, as it says in scripture? Horsley contends that what dominates the text (even taking account of the citations of prophetic texts) is not an apologetic purpose but the conflict between the newborn king of the Jews and the reigning king Herod which ultimately makes refugees of Jesus, Joseph and Mary as they attempt to escape the state terror enacted by Herod in 2.16-18. Such readings present a refreshed political edge to the text by highlighting how conflict with unjust political systems and structures is integral to its narrative.

Expanding the Roman Imperial Context

Exploration of further ways in which Matthew's Gospel reflects opposition to Rome's claims to sovereignty over the entire world was provided in a collection of essays edited by David Sim and John Riches in 2005. The book sought to make progress in three main areas of enquiry: first, into the very nature and behaviour of empires as they function as political realities; second, into the ways in which groups and individuals reacted towards the Roman Empire; and third, into the ways in which Matthew's Gospel specifically reflects attitudes towards Rome and Roman power.

The introduction to the volume situates the Matthean community within its historical context, namely, the traumatic aftermath of the events of 70 CE, during which Roman forces invaded Jerusalem and destroyed the Jewish temple. Given the loss of the temple and its cult, new markers of Jewish religious identity were beginning to materialize in differing contexts. The chapters cover a significant area of terrain, from introducing methods and theories for interpreting 'empire' as a political system, to Rome in Matthew's Gospel as well as other literature in and outside the New Testament. The book is helpful in demonstrating how Matthew's story of Jesus presumes in many ways the Roman occupation of Palestine, the traditional Jewish homeland.

Contributors to this volume tend to identify a more complex relationship to Roman imperialism in Matthew than simply the 'counternarrative' view introduced above. The Roman Empire provided both advantages and disadvantages for its subjects, and a multifaceted and perhaps contradictory (and sometimes ambivalent) attitude towards Rome was likely. Determining Matthew's specific views of the Roman Empire is difficult given that both positive and negative statements can be found in his Gospel. Moreover, it is difficult to determine how much the Christological and theological language of the Gospel is intended to function as anti-language, as discussed above. Given the malleability of language, such interpretations are driven in part by the hermeneutical presuppositions we bring to the text. It is possible to read the text in an anti-imperial way just as it is possible to read it in support of imperial ambitions.

Jesus' healing of the centurion's servant in Mt. 8.5-13 has become a hotly debated text in recent years with different interpretations demonstrating the pro- and anti-imperial perspectives. Within the text, a centurion (a Roman soldier in command of a hundred men) approaches Jesus and humbles himself as he requests the healing of his paralyzed servant. Jesus responds that 'in no one in Israel have I found such faith' (8.10). It is noted that the centurion is an agent and enforcer of imperial power and so Jesus has no choice but to obey the directives given to him. Does this mean that the centurion's affirming response in 8.8 ('Lord, I am not worthy to have you come under my roof…') is an empty gesture? Likewise, is Jesus' commendation of the centurion's example of faith genuine or is he simply paying homage to an enforcer of the law? The text, it would appear, supports multiple readings.

Social-Scientific Approaches

To probe further into the social and cultural structures encoded within the text, most scholars writing on the topic of Matthew's Gospel and Roman imperialism have relied heavily on social-scientific biblical criticism. This methodology became popular during the second half of the twentieth century as an extension of the dominant historical-critical approaches and brought insights from the disciplines of sociology and anthropology (cultural and historical) to the academic study of the Bible. Social-scientific approaches usually employ one or more models to understand and explain various cross-cultural phenomena within a biblical text. Such models are typically based on generalizations and/or theories from the social sciences and are intended to aid in the historical and literary interpretation of a text.

Social-scientific biblical criticism has been employed to explore a variety of topics within Matthew's Gospel in recent years. Prominent studies have included the analysis of the Matthean Jesus and deviancy, the important cultural categories of honour and shame and even the performance of Jesus' masculinity. Stuart Love (2009) employs social-scientific biblical criticism to discuss the interactions between Jesus and so-called 'marginal' women, as determined by the gender-specific social stratification that characterized the ancient Mediterranean context in which the text was produced. Another significant contribution has been that of Jerome H. Neyrey (1998), who places Jesus in his social and cultural context by measuring him against the 'pivotal values' of honour and shame in the ancient Mediterranean world. More will be said on this topic in the next chapter with regards to the construction of Jesus' masculinity in Matthew.

An important contribution of social-scientific analysis that makes a prominent appearance in the empire studies approach to Matthew's Gospel is the concept of the household (*oikia*/*oikos*). This is because the institution in the first century was not only rife with distinctions in roles based on gender, age and class, but also modeled as a microcosm of the wider imperial structuring of society. The emperor was seen as the father of the fatherland, and other households were modeled on the hierarchical structures that permeated the

Roman Imperial world. Michael H. Crosby pioneered the research into this topic in 1988 by employing a combination of historical, literary and then emerging social-scientific tools to explore the socio-economic environment of the Gospel's context. He observed how the household provides a unifying theme within Matthew and indicates a concern for social justice within urban-based communities. Within the Roman Empire, the household served as the basis and model unit for social and cultural life as well as the wider economic and political life within the Roman Empire. In terms of its members, it would encompass the immediate and extended family, slaves, servants and other workers, as well as tenants and so on. On a material level, it included the property and the building itself, in addition to any means of production.

The most recent work which best demonstrates the social-scientific methodology in relation to the Gospel of Matthew as outlined above is Dennis C. Duling's *A Marginal Scribe: Studies in the Gospel of Matthew in a Social-Scientific Perspective* (2012). It draws together and augments insights that Duling has developed over more than two decades of reading the Gospel of Matthew through a social-scientific lens. As its title suggests, it explores the Gospel and its characters through the prism of marginality, a category which Duling examines in significant depth and which he associates with the scribe responsible for the compilation of diverse texts and traditions into the Gospel in the context of empire. In such a context, he argues, the marginal scribe seeks to honour Jesus as Son of David in a way that is particular to the Gospel of Matthew.

Another important category of social-scientific analysis within the empire studies approach to Matthew's Gospel is that of social stratification. This is because social-scientific criticism is interested in exploring the social and cultural 'location' of the language of a text and the type of social and cultural world that the language evokes and creates. Most biblical scholars tend to refer to the work of Gerhard Lenski on social stratification in advanced agrarian societies. Lenski (1966), influenced by Marxist theorists, proposes a vertical model indicating social and economic status from the small ruling elite at the top to the much poorer and expendable classes on the bottom. The Roman Empire was an aristocratic empire; this means that a small elite of about two to three percent of the population ruled over the rest.

This ruling elite were in a position to shape the social experience of the empire's inhabitants (an estimated sixty to sixty-five million), not only determining their quality of life but also exploiting their labour for the control of wealth and to support their high and luxurious lifestyles. Those at the top of the pyramid were able to command a higher level of power, privilege and prestige, while those towards the bottom functioned to sustain and maintain the ruling elite's way of life. The highest stratum consisted of rulers (the emperor followed by other members of the governing class). Beneath them was a retainer class made up of those functionaries who served the ruling elite: scribes, soldiers and priests. Below them were the merchants, peasants and artisans. At the bottom were the expendables: prostitutes, bandits, the lame and disabled.

Roman Characters in the Gospel of Matthew

The most visible characters of Roman imperialism in Matthew's Gospel are the Roman soldiers (*stratiotai*) who are stationed in Palestine as part of the military occupation. These soldiers perform the tasks that more senior characters (such as centurions and kings) order them to carry out (cf. Mt. 2.16; 9.9; 14.10; 22.7; 27.26, 31-38). Centurions (*hekatontarchoi*) are also prevalent within the Matthean text. They function as leaders over detachments of one hundred soldiers and so wield considerable authority and power. The appearance of centurions in Mt. 8.9 and 27.54 symbolizes the oppressive Roman occupation of Palestine after 70 CE.

Pilate (27.2-66; 28.11-15) is the Roman governor and is probably the most powerful political figure in the Gospel. He is introduced specifically as 'the governor' (27.2), thereby emphasizing his military and political authority. It is the emperor, however, who stands at the very top of the Roman military and political hierarchy of the imperial social order. Within Matthew's Gospel, the emperor is relegated to an offstage role; nonetheless, his considerable power is referenced a number of times. For example, the most obvious impact that the emperor has on the lives of everyday peasants is that he taxes them—coins bear the image and the title of the emperor (22.19-20). The emperor was thought to embody the empire's patriarchal (male dominated) and androcentric (male centred) ideals and was proclaimed the 'Father of the Fatherland' (*pater patriae*).

Although such a model potentially oversimplifies class distribution (for there are further variables by which people are ranked: gender, family, ethnicity and so on), it is nonetheless helpful in gaining an appreciation for the political and social world in which the Matthean community was engaged. Are the perspectives presented within the Gospel directly at odds with those propagated by Rome, or do they accommodate and/or mimic the system of attitudes, values, dispositions and norms of the dominant imperial culture?

Those seeking an introduction to this aspect of New Testament and Matthean studies would do well to consult Warren Carter's guide, *The Roman Empire and the New Testament: An Essential Guide* (2006).

Critical Issues

Some scholars have expressed hesitation with regard to the intense focus on Roman imperialism in New Testament studies, particularly when the

Gospels are viewed simply as counter-imperial documents. We have seen how the Matthean text can be read in a number of different ways, using different methodologies and critical perspectives, and so such readings must be carefully nuanced against observations that the Bible has also been used to sanction war, colonialism and other imperial projects. For instance, the great commission at the end of Matthew's Gospel—'Go therefore and make disciples of all nations, baptizing them in the name of the Father and the Son and of the Holy Spirit' (28.19)—is tied to a strong tradition of European colonialism packaged in the discourse and impetus of worldwide Christian evangelism.

Furthermore, attempts to detoxify, rescue and/or redeem the text often mask underlying hermeneutical assumptions with regards to the authority of the text. The works of Carter, Duling, and others are based on a deeply confessional stance that is not always explicitly outlined. Given that the context behind the production of much of this scholarship was a time of neo-conservative Republican political hegemony within the USA, this stream of scholarship is often drawn into contemporary political debates because of the significant role the Bible plays in the public life of the USA.

Horsley is one scholar who explicitly links his broader work on counter-imperialism and the New Testament to contemporary American political life. Many citizens of the USA, he argues, understand their corporate identity not only in relation to Jesus but also in relation to Rome. The founding fathers of the USA conceived of the Constitution as establishing a new Republic in imitation of ancient Rome. One only has to observe the architecture of state buildings and civic space in the national capital, Washington, DC, to see the intentional resemblance to ancient Rome. Horsley further emphasizes the emergence of the USA as the world's only remaining superpower, following the collapse of the Soviet Union. Its dominance in economic and political affairs beyond its own borders, in addition to its heavy militarization and foreign interventions, leads Horsley and others to draw direct comparisons between the *pax Romana* (Roman peace) at the height of its empire and the contemporary situation of what Horsley labels the *pax Americana*.

Even so, the Matthean text appears to point to a complex variety of stances regarding Roman imperial domination. This suggests the importance with which we ought to declare our hermeneutical assumptions, not necessarily to undermine our position but rather to solidify our reading strategy. As we will see in the next chapter, a critical distance is required toward so-called 'objective' readings that attempt to mask their agendas, if one does not want to reinscribe today potential abusive and/or oppressive textures within the Matthean text. Indeed, the biblical text itself was used to provide an ideological basis for a new empire from Constantine onwards, and it still functions reasonably comfortably as an imperial text in many quarters of church and society today. It will be helpful for your further study of the Gospel of Matthew if you can begin to locate yourself on the map this chapter has laid out; context and its impact on the meaning of the text does not remain in the first century but continues into all contemporary interpretations of the text in context.

Chapter 4

Reading the Matthean Narrative with/in Contemporary Contexts

One of the key characteristics of Matthean scholarship within biblical studies generally during the past 15 years has been the range of hermeneutical or interpretive perspectives that have been utilized in the reading of the text. While it was made clear in the discussion in our Chapter 2 that each interpreter brings a particular hermeneutic or reading lens to the interpretive task, not all interpreters are explicit in identifying their hermeneutic. Nevertheless, there is a diverse group of contemporary biblical scholars who are contributing to the development of very clearly articulated reading perspectives. In this chapter, we will explore five of these reading perspectives and the contributions that they have made to a reading of the Gospel of Matthew: feminist, masculinity, queer, postcolonial and ecological (together with some combinations of two or more perspectives). Attention will also be given to the ways in which hermeneutics and choice of biblical methodology or methodologies combine to guide interpretation of texts.

In his second edition to *What are They Saying about Matthew* (1996), Donald Senior recognizes the contribution that feminist scholars have made and are making to the study of the Matthean Gospel since the publication of the first edition of this book in 1983. He names such scholars as Janice Capel Anderson, Celia Deutsch, Jane Kopas, Amy-Jill Levine, Pheme Perkins, Jane Schaberg, Antoinette Wire and Elaine Wainwright. Also, in 1995, Janice Capel Anderson published a substantial review of Matthean literature—'Life on the Mississippi: New Currents in Matthean Scholarship'—and she too drew attention to not only emerging feminist interpretations of the Gospel of Matthew but also the expanding range of hermeneutical approaches. The subsequent decade and a half has seen this material extend its reaches and it is this extension that we now map more closely.

Feminist Readings

A feminist reading perspective and ideology is located within feminism as a social movement for the human rights of women and an ideological critique of patriarchal power relations in society. It is concerned primarily with the ways in which gender is constructed asymmetrically in wider society, but also in texts that are, of course, produced and consumed within particular social and cultural contexts.

Gender, as the social construction of male and female, has been the key analytical tool within a feminist hermeneutic. It has been accompanied by the recognition that this social construction has not only shaped mindsets but also social and cultural structures and beliefs to facilitate the domination of men over women (patriarchy), or the domination of some men and some women over other men, women and children on the basis of class and race (kyriarchy). These categories intersect with class, race and other distinguishing features among women and have functioned in feminist readers' critical engagement with the text and in their interpretation of it. One of the things that we have already alluded to is the distinction between hermeneutic and methodology. Feminist interpreters combine their particular feminist perspective/s with a choice of biblical methodologies from within the wide range available to them. And so an analysis of gender and power in the Gospel of Matthew, for example, might intersect with narrative questions of character, plot and settings. It is this interrelationship of hermeneutic and methodology which will characterize the analysis of feminist readings which follows.

Even though its appearance was just outside the timeframe of this study, we want to turn our attention initially to the first, full-length feminist study of Matthew's Gospel (Wainwright 1991). It demonstrates clearly the hermeneutical and methodological intersections that characterize feminist readings. In abbreviated form it appeared as the commentary on Matthew in the second volume of *Searching the Scriptures* edited by Elisabeth Schüssler Fiorenza (1994); this abbreviated version may be more accessible to some readers.

Wainwright identifies 'liberation' and 'inclusion' as two critical lenses that characterize her particular feminist approach, the key being 'inclusion'. Since this was the first major feminist interpretation of the Gospel of Matthew, her focus was on the women characters—their inclusion in the text and their inclusion in the history of the text.

Methodologically, Wainwright combines both historical and narrative critical approaches in the overall work while recognizing the integrity of each. At a Stage One level of analysis, 'Inclusion in the Text', she undertakes a narrative critical reading that gives attention to the female characters as they are developed and function in the Matthean story. From this, she recognizes a significant 'understory' of women's engagement with Jesus' life and mission as narrated in the Matthean Gospel (1.3, 5, 6, 16; 18-25; 2.11,13, 14, 21, 22; 8.14-15; 9.18-26; 14.3-5; 15.21-28; 20.20-23; 26.6-13, 69, 71; 27.19, 55-56, 61 and 28.1-10). This is, Wainwright claims, an understory that is in tension with the dominant narrative and its patriarchal constructions. We invite readers at this point to read this narrative line in the Matthean Gospel as many of the studies discussed below will engage one or other of these texts.

Wainwright's Stage Two analysis, 'Inclusion in the Formation of the Text', is informed by a redaction critical study of the key texts listed above, demonstrating how women of the Matthean community may have been engaged in the shaping of the stories in which women are key characters. In the concluding Stage Three section, 'Inclusion within History', Wainwright uses historical criticism and the growing body of studies of women in the Greco-Roman world in dialogue with the previous two stages of textual analysis to reconstruct women's participation in the Matthean community within the first-century Jesus movement, an aspect of Matthean scholarship which had, until that time, been completely ignored. Wainwright's work makes a significant contribution to Matthean studies and demonstrates well how hermeneutic and methodology combine in interpreting the text.

Feminist readings are not, however, confined to texts in which women function as characters. Emily Cheney (1996) establishes reading strategies for women who are alienated by the patriarchal and androcentric aspects of the Gospel text. Her critical lens is that of gender, both male and female, as both function in the gendering of the Matthean text. She, therefore, extends the parameters of feminist readings of Matthew. She is particularly concerned with how women today, aware of the effect of dominant male gendering in narratives, read those texts of the Matthean Gospel in which characters are predominantly male. Her focal texts are, therefore, the commissioning of disciples (Mt. 10.5-15 and 28.16-20), the opening critique of the Scribes and Pharisees (23.1-12) and the meal with the twelve (26.20-29).

In developing her feminist perspective, Cheney dialogues with feminist literary critics (such as Elaine Showalter and Judith Fetterley) together with a range of other critical theorists. From this dialogue, three reading strategies emerge: (1) gender reversal, (2) analogy and (3) female characters as exchange objects. Her feminist hermeneutic combines seamlessly with new literary critical methodologies in her reading of the above texts through the lens of each of her reading strategies. A key feature of her work is that it profitably demonstrates how feminist readings need to be brought to bear on the entire text of the Gospel of Matthew, and not just those in which women function as key characters. She also extends the field of dialogue with critical theory in the development of feminist critique. These two features will characterize feminist readings of Matthew in subsequent years.

Appearing in the same year as Cheney's work was that of Celia Deutsch. Titled *Lady Wisdom, Jesus, and the Sages: Metaphor and Social Context in Matthew's Gospel* (1996), it looks at the metaphor of Sophia or Wisdom in Matthew's interpretation of Jesus. She does not explicitly name her work as feminist or develop a feminist framework for reading in this work, although in a later article—'Jesus as Wisdom: A Feminist Reading of Matthew's Wisdom Christology', which was included in *A Feminist Companion to Matthew* (2001) to be discussed below—she does clearly engage a feminist approach. We have included her book-length study here, however, because the metaphor of Sophia has been given significant scholarly attention by feminist scholars of the wisdom literature as well as that of early Christianity. Indeed, in 1994, just prior to Deutsch's work, Elisabeth Schüssler Fiorenza published a feminist reading of Jesus under the title, *Jesus—Miriam's Child, Sophia's Prophet: Critical Issues in Feminist Christology* (1994), in which the Sophia imagery in Matthew's Gospel receives very brief attention.

Returning to Deutsch's study, we note that she herself indicates awareness of feminist scholarship in relation to Sophia, and that her study of the Matthean use of the metaphor of Sophia is undertaken in a way that would be familiar to feminist scholars. She does not, however, develop a specific hermeneutic. Rather, she designates her approach methodologically as a combination of redaction and composition criticism that is attentive also to insights from literary criticism and the social-scientific approach. Her opening chapter demonstrates the potential for familiarity with the metaphor of Lady Wisdom in the Matthean community by looking at the metaphor in biblical, Second Temple and Tannaitic Judaism. She then explores a number of texts in which the metaphor is transformed: Mt. 8.18-22; 11.2-13.58; 23.34-36, 37-39. From this she concludes that many of the characteristics of Lady Wisdom are ascribed to Jesus in the Matthean narrative—a significant extension of understandings of the Matthean characterization of Jesus. In a subsequent chapter she develops this relationship, drawing the conclusion that the metaphor authorizes Jesus as a legitimate interpreter of the Torah. Later in the book she returns to the texts noted above (which she designates as 'Wisdom passages') to study how the disciples are portrayed. As a result of her study, she modestly claims that only in Mt. 11.19 and perhaps in 11.28-30 is Jesus explicitly identified with the Lady Wisdom figure of the Jewish Scriptures but that the metaphor colours other significant texts. While affirming the beauty of the metaphor she decries its use to legitimate an 'all-male collective leadership' (including that of Jesus) so that the female aspects of the metaphor disappear.

Wainwright (1998) continues to develop the two strands highlighted earlier: (1) ongoing dialogue with critical theory in the development and refining of feminist hermeneutics and (2) the extension of focal texts and themes being studied. She explores the category of 'difference' in her study of the Matthean construction of Jesus. This study takes account of the strong trend in Matthean scholarship to examine the Jesus of this Gospel by way of titles, as demonstrated in Senior's 1996 overview of scholarship that we discussed in our Introduction. Unlike these previous studies, however, a focus on 'difference' suggests that just as difference characterizes every community so too it can be explored in the Matthean community. Indeed, it is a feature already identified strongly in studies of the Matthean text. Scholars have highlighted conflicting positions in the Matthean text in relation to Judaism, Gentiles, the law, leadership and authority, and other issues. Wainwright argues that there were different communities of interpretation—different households—beneath the umbrella of what we call 'the Matthean community', and that these different readers or readership groups would have heard and understood the Jesus characterized in the Matthean Gospel in a range of different ways.

In order to engage with the meaning-making processes in relation to Jesus within these diverse Matthean households, Wainwright develops an approach to the text that characteristically combines a critical hermeneutics of suspicion with the reconstructive and creative/interpretive stage of reclamation, while using difference as well as gender as her analytic keys. Methodologically, she uses a socio-rhetorical approach that combines social-scientific, literary and ideological tools for analysis. Hermeneutic and methodology combine in what she calls an 'en-gendered reading'. This provides her with the tools to carefully examine the rhetoric of the Matthean stories of Jesus together with their encoding of the ways they might have functioned in the socio-cultural world of the first century.

Using this carefully constructed framework, she reads the Jesus of Matthew's Gospel through a selection of what she calls 'soundings': Matthew 1–2 ('Of Rachel's Lineage—Endangered Child/Liberated Liberator'); Mt. 11.1-30 ('Wisdom is Justified: Doing her Deeds and Bearing her Yoke'); Mt. 15.21-28 and 16.13-20 ('As She Desired and He Confessed—Boundary Walker and Deconstructive Builder'); and Mt. 27.32-28.20 ('The Liberator Liberated, the Crucified One Raised'). This study by Wainwright confirms Senior's final claim concerning Matthean Christology in his revised and expanded edition of *What are They Saying?* (1996): Matthew's presentation of Jesus goes beyond titles, categories and all our ways of reading them. Difference and an-other-ness can function to ensure that multiple voices be heard when making meaning of the Gospel story and its central character, Jesus.

One of the signs of the significant development of an approach within a discipline, whether it is hermeneutical or methodological, is the appearance of a collection of essays devoted to it. Feminist biblical studies in general and feminist studies of the Gospel of Matthew in particular are no exceptions. Such feminist collections emerged first in relation to books or sections of the Hebrew Bible and were edited by Athalya Brenner. Volumes on the New Testament appeared later. In 2001, Amy-Jill Levine as the key editor of the series, *Feminist Companion to the New Testament and Early Christian Writings*, produced its first volume on Matthew. The volume contains six articles that had already been published elsewhere and five that were written explicitly for this volume. Levine's introduction to the volume (2001a) situates the articles well within the context of Matthean studies in general and feminist Matthean studies in particular. Here, therefore, we will undertake a very brief survey of those articles in order to demonstrate their contribution to this developing field of feminist readings of the Gospel of Matthew.

Janice Capel Anderson's opening essay, 'Matthew: Gender and Reading' is, as Levine pointed out, a catalyst in feminist studies of Matthew. First appearing in 1983, it introduces the critical category of gender to a reading of the Matthean Gospel in dialogue with feminist literary critics. That lens is then turned to a reading of the androcentric or male-centred perspective of the Gospel as well as the female characters. Anderson's article thus opened the way for much of what has emerged in the interim three decades.

Julian Sheffield introduces a new topic into the feminist study of Matthew's Gospel: the uses of and references to the 'F/father'. She demonstrates by way of a careful study of terminology that the term is used as a key metaphor for God in a way that displaces earthly paternity. Indeed, she would claim that earthly fathers are discredited and their role replaced in the Gospel of Matthew by a newly constituted kinship structure. Some feminist scholars would bring a sharper critique to the 'father' metaphor because of its embeddedness in imperial Roman imagery of the emperor as well as the patriarchal family structure. With such a critique recognized, however, the reclamation that Sheffield proposes can contribute to a feminist critical rereading of a key Matthean metaphor.

The inclusion of Amy-Jill Levine's article, 'Discharging Responsibility: Matthean Jesus, Biblical Law, and the Haemorrhaging Woman' (2001b), introduces a critical consideration in not only feminist studies of the Gospel of Matthew but also feminist biblical studies and indeed all biblical studies, namely that of an anti-Jewish bias. She demonstrates ways in which the women of Jesus' day and women within first-century Judaism can be constructed quite negatively by feminist scholars in their process of reclaiming Jesus as a liberator of women in the Gospel. She does this by demonstrating the ways that Jewish purity laws are evoked, especially in relation to the story of the woman with a haemorrhage and that of the daughter of the synagogue leader (Mt. 9.18-26). Her critique has opened the way for some excellent studies of Jewish menstrual laws by Jewish scholars. These studies can now inform feminist and other interpretations of Gospel texts (see Cohen 1991; Fonrobert 1997).

The fourth essay in the *Feminist Companion* is Celia Deutsch's discussion of the metaphor of Wisdom and how this is used to characterize Jesus in the Gospel of Matthew. While the discussion in this essay is brief in comparison with her book-length study discussed above, she considers in this essay what the metaphor might tell us of women's experience in the

Matthean community. She decries that the Gospel does not tell us anything directly of this experience, but further examination of the metaphor in dialogue with the presence of women within the Gospel narrative leads her to suggest more strongly than in her book that the metaphor may have functioned negatively for women as it affirmed the teaching role of Jesus and the male disciples.

The next three articles focus on what has become a key text in feminist readings of Matthew's Gospel: the story of the Canaanite woman (Mt. 15.21-28). We will not address these here, as we will focus explicitly on this text at the end of this section. Rather, we turn now to Anthony Saldarini's article, 'Absent Women in Matthew's Households'. He raises the question in response to Wainwright's reading against the grain of the text and community in *Shall We Look for Another?* about why women are not more readily visible in the Matthean narrative. Saldarini turns his attention particularly to Matthew 18–20 and reads that text from a social-scientific perspective and within the socio-cultural context of first-century Judaism and emerging Christianity. He demonstrates that households are a central concern of these texts and that the Matthean Gospel re-envisages the household but does not address women's place within this reshaping. This question, then, is left to contemporary interpreters' re-imagining.

In the article 'Got into the Party After All: Women's Issues and the Five Foolish Virgins', Marie-Eloise Rosenblatt examines 'conventional' and 'artistic' readings of a Matthean parable which has received no prior feminist analysis. She isolates some of the problematic aspects of Mt. 25.1-13 in relation to its dualistic characterization of women within patriarchy (wise/foolish) as well as the absence of the bride from the narrative. Having made these moves that are typical of a hermeneutics of suspicion within a feminist analysis, however, Rosenblatt offers what she calls a 'redemptive reading'. She suggests that this parable envisages polemical situations in the community, especially among women, and that the redactor uses the two groups of women in the parable to address the polemic. The parable should be read then not only in relation to women but also the community as a whole; it addresses behavior that needed attention and correction, and it affirms what she calls 'theological moments' that are having a positive effect.

The two closing articles address the same text: the women's visit to the tomb in Mt. 28.1-10, and especially the question as to what the women are doing there. Thomas R.W. Longstaff titles his article 'What Are Those Women Doing at the Tomb of Jesus? Perspectives on Matthew 28.1', and Carolyn Osiek hers 'The Women at the Tomb: What Are They Doing There?' Longstaff reads the text through the lens of the Jewish custom of visiting the tomb of loved ones to keep watch up to the end of the third day in order to prevent premature burial. For him, therefore, it is not unusual that they are there. Osiek uses a redaction- critical approach to the text, but she also pays attention to sociological issues before turning to a feminist analysis. She concludes that the stories are less about proof than about meaning; they point not only to the 'absence' of Jesus but also the memory of the role of women.

This edited volume examined above clearly marks a significant point of development in feminist readings of the Gospel of Matthew. It demonstrates the complex range of categories of analysis that constitute a feminist reading, whether they be women, gender, male power, metaphor and many others. These are combined with an equally varied range of methodological approaches, including concern for metaphor, narrative, redaction, social categories, social-scientific analyses, and a range of combinations of these. The work highlighted here has continued and been combined with other hermeneutical approaches as the first decade of the twenty-first century unfolded, contributing further to the variety of approaches to the study of the Matthean Gospel and to our understanding of the text in contemporary contexts.

Discipleship has been a contentious issue in relation to women in the Gospels, that of Matthew being no exception. Scholars such as Talvikki Mattila (2002) began, at the turn of the millennium, to turn a critical lens on this issue. She explores discipleship in the Matthean text as have other Matthean scholars. Her feminist perspective, however, leads her to focus on 'power' in a way that other studies of Matthean discipleship do not. Narratives delineating 'power-over' are critiqued while those demonstrating 'power-with' are explored for potential meaning-making in contemporary communities of interpretation. In this regard she, like other feminist scholars, engages feminist critical theory as well as biblical methodologies, bringing together a narrative approach with limited historical considerations. She too moves beyond the pericopes in which women appear as characters, considering instead the movement of the entire story: its stories of women, of male disciples and of the crowds. She does not seek to make claims to women's full power or full oppression in the first century, but to highlight the movements within and across the power grid of both male and female characters in the Matthean narrative. In this she makes a significant new contribution to the study of discipleship in the Gospel of Matthew; by focusing on relationships rather than domination and control, she searches for clues of an 'inclusive following'—a characteristic of the *basileia* vision—in the Gospel of Matthew.

The study of Baby Parambi, *The Discipleship of the Women in the Gospel according to Matthew: An Exegetical Theological Study of Matt 27:51b-56, 57-61 and 28:1-10* (2003) is not undertaken from a feminist perspective. Indeed, he does not identity his hermeneutic so readers have to try to discern it through attention to his scholarly choices and emphases. We include his study here, however, as it focuses on passages with female characters, as Wainwright, Mattila, Longstaff and Osiek have done in detail. Parambi names his approach as 'exegetical, theological and biblical rhetorical'; although he calls his study 'unique', he offers no explanation of just exactly what constitutes his methodological approach and how his study is unique in the face of both the general as well as the feminist studies of women's discipleship in the Gospel of Matthew.

In an initial chapter, Parambi draws on studies of the roles and status of women in the Graeco-Roman world and emerging Christianity to reconstruct the place of women in the Matthean community. He does not engage with any analytical categories such as 'gender', 'power', 'representation', 'construction of difference' or the many others that have emerged from two decades of feminist and gender studies generally and of the biblical/Matthean text in particular. Nor has he, at this initial stage of his study, engaged the Matthean text. What he concludes, therefore, is idealized against a background of negative constructions of women in the Old Testament, inter-testamental literature and Hellenistic Judaism. He claims that women are portrayed as equal to men in the teachings of Jesus and the Pauline literature.

Parambi's study of the texts in which women are key characters in Matthew's narrative prior to the passion account leads him to conclude that while women play a significant role, they are neither characterized as nor called disciples. Such a claim, of course, depends on how one defines discipleship and so it is no surprise that the women at the cross are shown to exhibit only 'certain discipleship qualities' (Parambi 2003: 134). Parambi's two categories of being named 'disciple' and being called by Jesus prevent women from being among the leadership group. He places them in the next circle around Jesus. What he does not address is how such a placement represents what he claims as Jesus' liberating vision, teaching and action in relation to women. His study demonstrates, especially from within a feminist paradigm, that lack of attention to one's hermeneutic and to carefully articulated methodological approaches weaken one's arguments and claims.

The reprinting of a work is generally a sign of its significant contribution to scholarship. That is certainly true for Jane Schaberg's *The Illegitimacy of Jesus: A Feminist Theological Interpretation of the Infancy Narratives*. It was first published in 1987 and then reprinted in 2006. Two articles by Schaberg frame her original work in the reprinted edition and they provide insight into the backlash that the original publication of her work evoked as well as her dialogue with scholars who have engaged her text. She demonstrates that feminist scholarship is engaged scholarship; it seeks to impact society and the *ecclēsia* as well as the academy and, at times, this impact is effective. In Schaberg's case, her book raises questions of women's scholarship, abuse of women, societal attitudes to illegitimacy and its effect on women as well as its effect theologically.

In her book, Schaberg undertakes a feminist critical reading of the Infancy Narratives of both Matthew and Luke. Her feminist perspective is informed by and in dialogue with feminist studies. This makes her alert to the experience of oppression and of power among women, especially sexual oppression and the way contemporary perspectives on this can enable a re-reading of an ancient text. This perspective informs her use of historical-critical methodology and enables her to examine the text of the infancy narratives in historical context as well as intertextually with not only Leviticus but also pre- and post-Gospel traditions about the illegitimacy of Jesus and virginal conception.

In her major chapter on Matthew's account of Jesus' origins, Schaberg first examines what the four women who shatter the Matthean genealogy have in common in the context of the patriarchal world that undergirded the genealogy and their sexual activity. This opens the way for her to consider the possibility of Mt. 1.16 as a reference to an illegitimate pregnancy, since this verse likewise shatters the pattern of the genealogy as do the references to the other four women. She turns then to her very careful and detailed study of Mt. 1.18-25—a study that is informed by an accompanying analysis of Deut. 22.23-27, Sir. 23.22-26 and Isa. 7.14. This leads her to conclude that Matthew links a tradition of Jesus' illegitimacy with that of divine begetting and Joseph's acceptance of the woman and her child. Read from a feminist perspective, God is one who sides with the 'endangered woman and child' but this woman and child are contained within a patriarchal narrative. She invites interpreters to listen for echoes of such themes in the unfolding Matthean narrative. While many feminist scholars of Matthew have engaged Schaberg's study in their readings of the infancy narrative (and she dialogues with their work in an epilogue to the anniversary edition), we are not aware of anyone specifically taking up her invitation. Her work remains, perhaps, the most radical feminist reading of a section of the Gospel of Matthew and the backlash against it in the academy and the church and in Shaberg's own personal life stands as a beacon in relation to engaged biblical hermeneutics, especially feminist hermeneutics which challenge personal, social and cultural identities and structures.

A Focus Text: Mt. 15.1-28

Often a particular biblical text can receive significant attention under the umbrella of a Gospel theme or within a hermeneutical approach. The text which has 'characterized' a feminist reading of Matthew's Gospel is Mt. 15.21-28, the story of the Canaanite woman's encounter with Jesus on behalf of her demon-possessed daughter. It will not be possible here to engage fully with this text or all of the emerging interpretations, as they are myriad. An overview, however, may point to why this text has attracted such attention.

A number of key Matthean themes intersect in Mt. 15.21-28 and it is because of this, perhaps, that it has gained such attention—a database search provided twenty-one entries (i.e. chapters of books or journal articles) on this pericope since 1995 and this list does not include all the book chapters. The text occurs at a strategic point in the middle section of the Gospel according to a number of structures. It presents Jesus' engagement with a woman named as Canaanite and this takes place outside or on the boundaries between Israel and its coastal neighbor, thus raising questions about ethnicity and the scope of Jesus' mission—to the Gentiles or only the house of Israel? This, in its turn, has potential for anti-Jewish interpretation, a concern in contemporary biblical scholarship and Matthean studies. That there are not one but two female characters in this short text, even though the daughter is generally overlooked by interpreters, provides material for a range of feminist interpretations, indeed one could suggest that work on this episode is almost synonymous with feminist Matthean scholarship.

A book-length study of this text is by Glenna S. Jackson (2002), who sees this story as being paradigmatic of faith and also of the proselytizing of a woman. She claims a feminist critique as underlying her study, although she does not delineate how she understands such a critique. Her methodology is historical-critical, giving particular emphasis to redaction criticism with a goal of contributing to further reconstruction of early Christianity.

An initial focus on the setting for the pericope in the district of Tyre and Sidon affirms the significance of the Jewish/Gentile tension in the Gospel. This is followed by a careful study of the background to and Matthean use of 'Canaanite' with both negative and positive connotations. From this, Jackson claims that Matthew's explicit introduction of the 'Canaanite' designation portrays the woman as a proselyte in line with the women of the genealogy whom Jackson has understood as proselytes. The Canaanite woman's gender, ethnic status and location all work together in this story to provide a paradigm not for Gentile mission, as is so often claimed, but for proselytism.

When discussing the *Feminist Companion to Matthew* earlier, we noted that it contains three articles on Mt. 15.21-28, the most dedicated to any particular section of the Gospel in this collection and indicative of the impetus that lead us to choose Mt. 15.21-25 as a focal text. Gail O'Day's article, 'Surprised by Faith: Jesus and the Canaanite Woman', was originally published in 1989 for what she calls both theological and pastoral outcomes. She recognizes the problems in the text that have confronted interpreters: namely, Jesus' refusal to respond to the woman; and the woman's refusal to go away. O'Day goes on to identify the story as the woman's story more than a story of Jesus, and then turns to the Lament Psalms as throwing light on the woman's pleas for her daughter. As the psalmists in the lament psalms are with God, so too she argues is the woman with Jesus, demonstrating a strong faith in God and a refusal to despair or to relent from their plea. O'Day claims, as her title suggests, that Jesus is 'surprised' by the woman's faith and her plea is granted.

Elaine Wainwright turns attention to the character in this story who is consistently read over or rendered invisible: the Canaanite woman's daughter. As her title, 'Not without my Daughter: Gender and Demon Possession in Matthew 15:21-28', suggests, she also gives attention to the demon possession of the daughter, thus identifying another theme that is likewise obscured in the discussions of this pericope, even though the theme is characteristic of Matthew as a whole. Gender continues as a focus but Wainwright employs a socio-rhetorical approach, so the demon possession as constructed in the Matthean text can be considered not only rhetorically but also socio-culturally. The overall study shows a correlation between demon-possession and ethnicity in the healing language of this pericope. In the chapter on Matthew's Gospel in Wainwright's *Women Healing/Healing Women: The Genderization of Healing in Early Christianity* (2006), this pericope is set in the context of women and healing.

Stephenson Humphries-Brooks's 'The Canaanite Wom*e*n in Matthew' sets the story of the Cannanite 'mother' into the context of the 'grandmother': *Rachab*, who appears in Mt. 1.5a. He emphasizes that the audience is intended to perceive Rahab as a sinner, as an exceedingly marginalized woman but one who belongs in Jesus' genealogy. For him, therefore, as for Jackson above, the designation of the woman of Mt. 15.21-28 as 'Canaanite' is very important. As a result of an examination of her encounter with Jesus, Humphries-Brooks draws some conclusions that others have likewise made: Jesus learns from the woman; she appears to be a better theologian, she wins a theological argument with him—and he does not forget her daughter and her healing. The third Canaanite woman he identifies in Matthew's Gospel is Herodias and he sees her as exemplary of the ills of patriarchy and phallocentricity. Her story ruptures the Matthean theological world and, like the other two Canaanite women, demands new readings.

We turn now to one last article that demonstrates the significance of Mt. 15.21-28, so you can follow up on additional ones that we are unable to treat here. Amy-Jill Levine's 'Matthew's Advice to a Divided Readership' (2001c) is cleverly titled for a collection of essays in memory of William G. Thompson, whose major work was *Matthew's Advice to a Divided Community*. Levine creatively sets up a dialogue between an 'older brother' (representative of the 'traditional' historical-critical scholarship and a belief that the meaning of the text lies in the first century) and a 'younger sister' (representative of more recent scholars approaching the text through a range of interpretive lenses). She uses scholarship on Mt. 15.21-28 to explore what she has designated as 'a divided readership'. Levine's is a creative approach but one that creates too stark a dichotomy. Given the scholarship that has been explored above, it is clear that many feminist scholars are using traditional historical-critical approaches, social-scientific methods, historical investigations as well as newer methodologies that have emerged across the discipline of biblical studies. What they bring anew to the discipline, as has been emphasized throughout this chapter, are contemporary reading perspectives. What the dichotomy fails to identify are the reading lens of all scholars, especially those who don't explicitly name their perspectives. Levine is right to warn against an anti-Jewish bias that can very readily characterize any reading of this pericope, but the dichotomy noted above needs to be read critically rather than descriptively. With Levine, however, we too would hope that scholars who have in the past interpreted and will in the future interpret this text will be able to engage creatively and in dialogue across methodological and hermeneutical approaches so Mt. 15.21-28 may be read with feminist approaches but many other approaches as well. The article by Veronica Koperski, 'The Many Faces of the Canaanite Woman in Matthew 15,21-28', in the recently published proceedings of the 2009 Colloquium Biblicum Lovaniense on the Gospel of Matthew begins with a consideration of Levine's article but then demonstrates more fully than we have been able to do here the significance of Mt. 15.21-28 in not only feminist but also Matthean studies generally.

Before turning to other reading perspectives, we conclude by calling readers' attention to Wainwright's 'Feminist Criticism and the Gospel of Matthew' in Powell's recent volume, *Methods for Matthew* (2009a). In that article she gives more attention than is possible here to elements of the feminist hermeneutic. Her interpretation of Mt. 27.57–28.15 demonstrates how such a hermeneutic informs one's chosen biblical methodology, in this instance a socio-rhetorical approach, in order to guide meaning-making and how this functions in relation to a specific text for interpretation.

Masculinity Readings/Reading Masculinity

Feminist studies, as they are developed, turn attention to the critical study of gender as a significant category. These in turn, open the way for men's and/or masculinity studies. Sensitive to the critiques of feminism, practitioners of men's studies noted that masculinity, like femininity, is a social construction that deserves critical study in its own right. As this field of study develops, it is sometimes linked with feminist studies under the umbrella of gender studies. As of yet, however, this area of study has had only minimal impact on biblical studies; and even less on Matthean studies.

One of the key collections of articles that does address the nexus of New Testament and masculinity studies is the Semeia Studies volume, *New Testament Masculinities*, edited by Stephen D. Moore and Janice Capel Anderson (2003). Two articles focus on Matthew's Gospel. In the first of these,

Jerome H. Neyrey's study, is entitled 'Jesus, Gender, and the Gospel of Matthew'. Known for his expertise in social-scientific approaches to Matthew, Neyrey employs models of the construction of Hellenistic masculinity by way of texts from the era, noting that places, roles, tasks and objects are divided according to gender. After establishing the male gendering of these categories, he reads the Jesus of Matthew's Gospel through this lens. The major category he examines is that of space, noting that males participate predominantly in the public life of the city as well as in certain private spaces, pointing out also that human sexual organs are public and private according to gender. In light of this, he examines Jesus within the public and private spaces in which the Gospel story unfolds. He particularly notes the extent of challenges to Jesus in public space as well as this as the space for most of his speech. Jesus is rarely characterized within a typical kinship structure. Neyrey has indicated through this study that attentiveness to masculinity and its construction in and through texts is a productive arena for New Testament and Matthean studies and that exploration of other categories that were highly engendered in antiquity will contribute significantly to such studies.

Moore and Anderson address the general issues of 'Matthew and Masculinity' and they, like Neyrey, recognize the need to establish the sex/gender structures of antiquity by analyzing ancient texts and their vocabulary. From this they note that the language of masculinity is strangely absent from the Matthean text. What they do note, however, is that the Gospel abounds in references to male kinship roles and relationships and the link between these and the household. It is these that they analyze through the Gospel under headings of genealogy, fathers, householders, brothers and eunuchs. As with Neyrey's article, Moore and Anderson simply provide a glimpse into an area of study that holds potential for much more development.

A significant critique is brought to these studies of masculinity in the Gospel of Matthew and the New Testament generally by one of the respondents to the *Semeia* volume, Maud W. Gleason. She notes that the evaluation of masculinity in the Matthean Gospel in the two articles discussed above takes place against a construction of ancient masculinity conceived in the context of the Mediterranean region generally. Insufficient attention has been given, she suggests, to such a construct in first-century Palestine at the extreme edge of the empire, influenced as it was by Jewish cultural codes as much as those of the empire. This is a task that remains for scholars to take up as masculinity readings are further developed. But before leaving this approach we note two further studies of masculinity in the Matthean Gospel.

Carmen Bernabé takes up the last issue that Moore and Anderson discuss: eunuchs in Matthew. She examines this issue in the context of Mt. 19.1-12 in an article entitled 'Of Eunuchs and Predators: Matthew 19:1-12 in a

Cultural Context', and demonstrates that first-century male honor was very clearly defined within the social code of masculinity by the type of relationships a man had with his wife. Jesus' evocation of the Genesis text rather than the Levitical position cited by the Pharisees challenges the codes of accepted masculinity within marriage, and in relation to divorce and adultery. In light of what she has established, Benabé understands Jesus' reference to eunuchs in 19.10-12 as symbolic of the loss of honour by those men who would actually take up his previous teaching and live it. Her work demonstrates that reading the Matthean text through the lens of masculinity and in dialogue with men's studies has much to offer Matthean studies and that the question is wide open. There is not yet a key study to demonstrate masculinity readings of the Gospel of Matthew.

Colleen Conway has taken one step further toward this by including a chapter on the Jesus of Matthew's Gospel in her study of Jesus' masculinity: *Behold the Man: Jesus and Greco-Roman Masculinity* (2008). She demonstrates how ideal Graeco-Roman masculinity is refracted through the Jewish scriptures and traditions in Matthew's characterization of Jesus. Jesus is a public speaker/teacher and yet he is characterized as a Wisdom teacher. While Wisdom is personified female in the Jewish scriptures, Conway argues that this is because young men are instructed to pursue the virtues that she represents: prudence, justice, courage and many more. Conway then demonstrates how the teachings of Jesus, refracted through the lens of wisdom, promote or proclaim ideal masculinity as demonstrated by Jesus and as required for disciples (we might note here that such an approach could be combined with the feminist reading of wisdom discussed above). The climax to her analysis is the final scene of the Gospel that, Conway claims, elevates Jesus beyond any Roman emperor on the 'masculinity/divinity gradient'. From this climactic point of Jesus epitomizing Graeco-Roman masculinity, she turns to an analysis of Jesus and 'marginal masculinities'. What she has demonstrated in relation to Jesus and masculinity is similar to many other aspects of the Matthean Gospel: the picture is complex and multi-dimensional with dominant images being critiqued or undermined by alternatives that likewise characterize the narrative. One could also bring to her work the critique of Gleason noted above.

Since the study of Matthew through the lens of 'masculinity' is in its infancy, there is no key text that has emerged. We turn, therefore, to a third hermeneutic which has links with gender and sexuality studies, namely queer hermeneutics.

Queer Hermeneutics

Another related hermeneutical approach to feminist criticism and masculinity readings that has been gaining some traction within the wider discipline of biblical studies is queer criticism. This approach has yet to take off in Matthean scholarship and only a few brief studies have appeared.

Queer criticism first emerged outside of biblical studies in the 1990s as an extension to and response to the feminist critique of patriarchy by identifying and exploiting the inherent instability of conventional categories of gender and sexuality. Its key feature is the recognition of heteronormativity as an oppressive social construct that assumes heterosexuality as the (often exclusive) norm to organize and structure system of sexual relationships. Within this construct, gender is thought to be biologically fixed and fits distinctly into two categories: male and female. A queer hermeneutic attempts to destabilize heteronormativity by exposing its contradictions and limitations, as well as pointing to possible instances of gender blurring in both texts and wider society. They argue that gender and sexuality are not fixed, stable and essentialist categories, but rather are social constructions that sustain oppressive power relations that exclude and perpetuate violence towards so-called 'deviant' sexual identities.

Current investigations into biblical masculinities have made little direct use of queer theory; instead, they tend to draw on scholarship in the classics that deals with codes and conventions. Although this data is crucial for an understanding of the construction and gendering of the ancient world, a narrow focus can potentially lead to the re-inscription of patriarchy and gender norms in the world in front of the text. As both a hermeneutics of suspicion and a hermeneutics of liberation, queer criticism has important implications for the interface between the modern and ancient worlds in our interpretation of the Gospel of Matthew.

Scholars undertaking queer studies propose that contemporary concepts of sexual orientation, for example, were unknown before the modern period, and that there were no clear terms for contemporary labels like 'homosexual', 'heterosexual' or 'bisexual' in ancient Mediterranean cultures. Moreover, an increasing number of scholars argue that ancient Greeks and Romans did not condemn homosexuality as such. Rather, they claim that certain sexual configurations within both same gender and opposite gender relationships were deemed 'unnatural': the real concern for ancient people was honour and shame, codes—introduced in the previous chapter—that regulated socio-sexual behaviour. For instance, they suggest that the shaming involved in male-male sexual intercourse, was the forfeiture of honour for (only) the penetrated partner (Lev. 18.22). Congruently, in their view, the ancient world did not construct gender identity as a strict binary model, but with both sexes on a single (androcentric) gender axis. The manliest man was situated at the top, with less masculine men below, followed by effeminate men, and finally women. In this respect, it was possible for a man to descend into the feminine realm, and, in exceptional cases, for a woman to rank higher than some of her male counterparts. These observations may have significant hermeneutical implications for our reading of gender and sexuality in the Gospel text and, further, they disrupt the dominant ideology of heteronormativity in the world before the text.

The most explicit example of queer criticism of the Gospel of Matthew can be found in *The Queer Bible Commentary* (2006) that provides a reading of the entire Gospel from a queer hermeneutical perspective. Its author, Thomas Bohache, combines what he calls an 'inclusive' hermeneutic with a combination of traditional historical-critical and literary methodologies in his reading of the text. In tandem with Warren Carter and Jerome Neyrey, he regards the imperial context as central in forming the Matthean community's marginal identity. This is a crucial aspect by means of which queer readers can identify with the text and its point of view. As a result, Bohache regards Matthew's Gospel as a liberatory text through which a queering and querying can bring out its full counter-cultural meaning.

As an example of what a queer reading of the Gospel might look like, it is useful to return once again to the beatitudes in Mt. 5.3-12. As we observed in Chapter 2, commentators are divided as to whether the beatitudes in Matthew are 'softer' or 'harder' than in Lk. 6.20-26. Does the Matthean text's spiritualizing language ('Blessed are the poor *in spirit*', Mt. 5.3) downplay or perhaps domesticate a more radical underlying message of social challenge and resistance? From a queer perspective, Bohache argues that the beatitudes function as coded language that differs in meaning depending on the context of its readers/hearers. The author of Matthew couches potentially revolutionary language in softer, more acceptable language, which is less offensive to the upholders of normalcy. Accordingly, the reader is invited to engage in the process of decoding the more radical messages hidden between the text's gaps. These inferences to a hidden counter-cultural kernel function much like sexual innuendo and can be penetrated with what Bohache labels 'homotextuality'.

Another noteworthy contribution is an article appearing in the *Journal of Biblical Literature*, co-authored by Theodore W. Jennings and Tat-Siong Benny Liew, entitled 'Mistaken Identities but Model Faith: Rereading the Centurion, the Chap, and the Christ in Matthew 8:5-13' (2004). While not explicitly employing a queer hermeneutic, it does present an unconventional reading of the well-known pericope concerning Jesus' healing of the centurion's servant. The authors, who are known for their queer approaches to other Gospel texts, contend that the dominant interpretation of this text is based on two mistakes or mistaken identities. First, readers make assumptions about the identity of the servant/boy upon whose behalf the centurion approaches Jesus for healing. For Jennings and Liew, the centurion's *pais* (often translated as 'servant') is in fact his 'boy-love' with whom he is engaged in a pederastic relationship. The authors support this contention with a critical exploration of the term's appearance across ancient

Greco-Roman culture and, in particular, within Roman military culture. Second, dominant interpretations mistake the centurion's understanding of the identity of Jesus. They suggest that the centurion mistakes Jesus not as the Son of God but as a commander of demons in a particular hierarchical chain that is part of the social ordering of first-century society which included the arrangement of sexual relationships. Jesus' willingness to grant the centurion's request implies for Jennings and Liew the affirmation of sexual 'deviants' in Matthew's Gospel.

Proponents of queer readings suggest that one must first be open to readings that might challenge received wisdom about what the Bible says about sexuality and gender. Queer critics argue that resistance to such proposals might in fact reveal underlying homophobia, an ailment of heteronormativity, which influences the hermeneutical filters of contemporary readers. A queer hermeneutic, therefore, seeks to transgress these constraints on biblical interpretation; doing so, in their view, may facilitate the possibilities for liberatory meaning-making in a reader's critical engagement with the text.

Postcolonial Hermeneutics

While gender has characterized the three hermeneutics discussed above and each in one way or another has also given attention to power, another hermeneutic has emerged in recent biblical scholarship whose focus has been predominantly on power, especially as it has functioned in contexts of colonial oppression. This has become known as postcolonial hermeneutic. Its foundational and most prolific proponent is R.S. Sugirtharajah. Beginning from the perspective of critiquing colonialism, it has moved to much more pervasive critiques of what might be called the aftermath of global colonization by powerful nations: displacement leading to global diasporas, the plight of the rural poor, the effects of the economic crisis across the world, to name but a few of the contexts that cry out for postcolonial readings of the Bible. In addition, postcolonial hermeneutic is beginning to interact with various hermeneutics we discussed earlier, however slowly. It should be noted, however, that it differs from the Empire Studies approach explored in Chapter 3, in that its critical analysis of contemporary structures of power informs a similar critique of the encoding of empire into the Matthean text. It is not simply a reading of the text in light of the imperial context but also a critique of the text's own imperialistic inclinations.

The work of Musa Dube (2000) is arguably most significant in postcolonial studies of Matthew's Gospel; this is affirmed by Fernando Segovia in his article, 'Postcolonial Criticism and the Gospel of Matthew' in *Methods for Matthew* (2009). Segovia's is the second article in that volume which addresses a hermeneutical perspective rather than a biblical methodological approach, the other being the article on feminist criticism by

Wainwright (2009a). As will become evident below, these two critical perspectives coalesce in Dube's work.

Segovia's article provides the newcomer to biblical studies with an excellent overview of postcolonial criticism, including how it has emerged within and been shaped by biblical studies as well as its impact on Matthean studies. In order to see such a study unfolding in relation to Matthew's Gospel, the reader should turn to Musa W. Dube's *Postcolonial Feminist Interpretation of the Bible* (2000). In her first chapter, she explores what she calls the 'postcolonial condition' and its 'subjects', entering into dialogue, as do other postcolonial theologians and biblical scholars, with the theorists of postcolonialism in literary and cultural studies internationally. She highlights focal issues such as land, race, power, the reader, international connection and, finally, gender. Hers is not just a postcolonial approach but a postcolonial feminist approach, which recognizes that all the focal issues are impacted by gender. In her second chapter she explores how the postcolonial condition intersects with feminisms to provide her with a frame for reading not only texts but also contexts.

From the above, Dube develops 'literary-rhetorical' methods to read the biblical text in a way that can 'resist and decolonize' both the gendered and imperial dominations encoded in the text. She draws on the new literary criticisms and socio-cultural criticism, but these are informed by her postcolonial optic. In this task, 'empire' becomes a significant category; this leads her to a set of questions in relation to 'political imperialism', travel, difference and gender representations that guide her feminist postcolonial readings. As with the feminist approach discussed above, her postcolonial reading seeks to critically uncover the representation of 'empire' in the text. Having done this, however, she reads the text in a way that can be heard as liberating for the colonized, especially women. She calls this aspect a rereading of the master's texts and a retelling of history. She demonstrates her approach initially through reading empire-building in and through the Exodus as narrative and event.

Dube's scholarship had been associated with Matthean studies before her book was published, because of an article, 'Readings of *Semoya*: Batswana Women's Interpretations of Matt 15:21-28', which was published in 1996. This same Matthean passage also receives significant attention in her book. From her postcolonial perspective she critically engages empire in the Gospel text before reading Mt. 15.21-28 through the 'reading prism' of Rahab—that is, a reading prism of imperial domination. Dube then critiques representative Western readings of Mt. 15.21-28: social-scientific, historical-critical, literary critical and white Western feminist readings (Dube also distinguishes these feminist readings in terms of methodology). Her critical lens leads her to ask whether the scholars she engages take seriously the imperial setting of Matthew; this enables her to demonstrate the need for both a gendered and an imperial lens. Hers is a radical critique and one that scholars, especially Matthean scholars, cannot ignore. She concludes her work by reading with the women of the African Independent Churches. She has provided one of the clearest and well-developed reading frameworks and practices within postcolonial and postcolonial feminist interpretations. Matthean scholars are fortunate that the text to which she gives most attention is that of the Gospel of Matthew; Dube's work becomes a challenge to any subsequent interpretation of the Gospel. Before leaving her work, it should be noted that she demonstrates most significantly what is a key characteristic of engaged readings: they shape directions in not only scholarship but also one's life.

Musa Dube seeks to create spaces in which women's voices can be heard, such as through her co-editing of collections of African biblical scholars: *'Reading With': An Exploration of the Interface between Critical and Ordinary Readings of the Bible: African Overtures* (1997); *Other Ways of Reading: African Women and the Bible* (1996); and, later, *The Bible in Africa: Transactions, Trajectories, and Trends* (2000), the first and last co-edited with Gerald West. She also brings her scholarship to address the HIV/AIDS challenges in Africa, as her co-edited work with Musimbi Kanyoro, *Grant me Justice! HIV/AIDS and Gender Readings of the Bible* (2004), and a number of articles attest.

Segovia also discusses Warren Carter's *Matthew and Empire* within his article on postcolonial criticism of the Gospel of Matthew, but he notes that Carter's approach is neither perspectival nor contextual (and so we have chosen to discuss it in Chapter 3). Carter does bring a more perspectival approach to his chapter on the Gospel of Matthew in *A Postcolonial Commentary on the New Testament Writings*, edited by Fernando Segovia and R.S. Sugirtharajah, but his predominant approach places him within the emerging Matthew and Empire (or the gospel and its imperial context) camp rather than a thorough postcolonial one.

Ecological Hermeneutics

Ecological hermeneutics is perhaps the most recent interpretive lens that scholars have brought to biblical studies in general and Matthew's Gospel in particular. It is connected to a growing concern with ecology and the preservation of Earth and its ecosystems. Like feminist approaches, it has emerged as a hermeneutical perspective from the social movement over ecology or the environment, and it began as a response to the concern that the Bible has been used to justify human exploitation of the environment. It has developed as a critical perspective in relation to not only the biblical text and its anthropocentric (human-centred) content but also a similar anthropocentrism characterizing conventional reading strategies of the biblical text and resulting interpretations. Interpreters using an ecological hermeneutic attempt to read against the grain of the text by directing attention to the Earth and its ecosystems as subjects within the text and not simply as background and/or scenery.

Those seeking an introduction to an ecological approach to the Gospel of Matthew should consult the recent article by Elaine Wainwright in *Biblical Interpretation*: 'Images, Words and Stories: Exploring Their Transformative Power in Reading Biblical Texts Ecologically' (2012b). This approach will be explained briefly and demonstrated in the following chapter through an ecological reading of the Matthean beatitudes. Wainwright has also published a number of articles (2009b; 2010; 2011; 2012a) on her way to writing a commentary on the Gospel of Matthew for the Earth Bible Commentary Series, currently being published by Sheffield Phoenix Press.

Conclusion

This chapter has drawn attention to those studies of the Matthean Gospel that have been shaped by specific hermeneutics. They have advanced Matthean scholarship significantly since 1995 and have, we hope, opened the way to more engaged readings of the Gospel into the twenty-first century as it unfolds.

Chapter 5

Readings the Matthean Beatitudes (Mt. 5.1-12) Ecologically

Blessed are… (Mt. 5.1-12).

Attention has already been given in this Guide to different ways that interpreters have read what are perhaps the most well-known verses in the Gospel of Matthew: the eight beatitudes. Each scholar's chosen methodological approach and/or hermeneutical lens have provided new and different insights into this familiar text. It is appropriate, therefore, that we turn one of the most contemporary hermeneutical lenses—the ecological—to these well-known verses of Mt. 5.1-12. In terms of methodology, we will do so socio-rhetorically. Before beginning the interpretation, however, we will explore more fully the ecological hermeneutic introduced in the previous chapter, as well as how it interacts with the socio-rhetorical methodology.

Ecological Hermeneutic and Methodology

A key characteristic of this interpretive framework is the shift in consciousness called for by Lorraine Code (2009). She names the new consciousness 'ecological thinking' and sees it as a radical shift from anthropocentrism (or human-centredness) that has dominated both thinking and practice (and hence biblical interpretation), at least in recent history.

An ecological hermeneutic, like the feminist, postcolonial and queer perspectives described in the previous chapter, is characterized by a critical approach to the text. Within the feminist, postcolonial and queer hermeneutics, that critique is focused on the human community and its issues concerning gender, sexuality and power. The emergence of an ecological hermeneutic recognizes that the human-centred focus of both text and interpretation needs to be uncovered. A second movement in the task of interpretation is, however, a reconfiguring of the text's interpretation so that the Earth as planet, with both human and other than human constituents, is foregrounded and considered together with the divine in the text. Such a hermeneutics of suspicion and hermeneutics of reconfiguring need to work together in an ecological reading.

A category of analysis that is particularly helpful to an ecological reading of a text and that is also grounded in the materiality of Earth is a focus on 'habitat'. This term refers to human and other than human interrelationships, as they all inhabit planet Earth. 'Habitat' holds together the material and the social, especially as these are encoded in the biblical text. This category can inform the methodological approach chosen for the interpretation of particular texts.

In this regard, we have chosen to use an adapted form of the socio-rhetorical approach that has been developed by Vernon Robbins. Narrative criticism with its attention to characters, setting, plot and other rhetorical features guides analysis of the inner texture of the text. Within an ecological reading, animal characters and referents, agricultural processes such as sowing seed and reaping the harvest, and weather features that include wind and rain are not just backdrop to the human/divine narrative but constitute 'habitat' as this is woven into the text's meaning-making. The intertexual or the texture woven between texts can be twofold. There are other texts that echo in the Matthean text. One example of such intertextuality is Mt. 1.23, which characterizes the Gospel and is rich in meaning with traces of Isa. 7.14 echoing through it. Also, the contemporary reader weaves into the text's interpretation current texts which might include, by way of example, ecological theories and categories. The significance of 'habitat' can guide both these interpretive movements.

Robbins recognizes a third texture that he calls the socio-cultural. It is appropriate to an ecological reading to extend this texture and name it ecological. Exploring this texture allows us to situate the social and cultural textures of the text, which are generally seen as related to humans only, within a broader framework of the intricate interrelationship of the other than human with the human—this, again, constitutes 'habitat'. Just as an analysis of socio-cultural textures turned attention to ways in which traces of first-century social and cultural features were encoded in the Matthean text, so too will an analysis of the ecological texture extend to ways in which first-century habitats, cosmology, geography and other ecological features are encoded in the text together with the social and cultural. Thus this third texture can rightly be named ecological. It is the exploration of the interrelationships within and between these three textures informed by ecological thinking that will guide the reading of Mt. 5.1-12 that follows.

Reading Mt. 5.1-12 Ecologically

As we turn our attention to Mt. 5.1-12, it needs to be located within the first Matthean discourse or the Sermon on the Mount (Matthew 5–7). This, in its turn, is linked narratively with a collection of healings (Mt. 8.1–9.34) by way of a frame constructed by parallel summary passages (4.23 and

9.35). Not only are place and proclamation intimately linked but proclamation (articulated now as teaching in their synagogues and proclaiming the good news of the *basileia* [4.23]) is also extended to include the healing of 'every disease and every sickness' (4.23 in parallel to 9.35). The summary passages direct the reader's focus to the named region of Galilee with all its material/geographic, socio-political and cultural features that were characteristic of the first century, as described by scholars such as Sean Freyne (2004), Mark Chancey (2005) and Richard Horsley (1996). This suggests to the reader that proclamation always occurs within the inter-con/textuality of habitat. Matthew 4.23 evokes all of this under the rubric of 'Galilee', but 9.35 makes more specific reference to the built environment of 'cities and villages', while both verses identify the 'synagogues' as the place in which teaching takes place. Jesus' reputation spreads, however, beyond the context of his ministry. It extends 'throughout all Syria', and great crowds 'follow', but these crowds are now not only from Galilee but 'the Decapolis, Jerusalem, Judea, and from beyond the Jordan'. The ministry of Jesus cannot be separated from the material—it has a habitat rich in material as well as social and cultural elements.

Already in the narrative, however, Jerusalem and Judea have been places of resistance to the infant Jesus' birth but also the object of John's proclamation of the *basileia* of the heavens/sky (3.1-2). The attentive reader will, therefore, be wary of hearing these extensive geographic claims of the narrator as necessarily acceptance of Jesus' proclamation and healing. They do, however, focus the reader's attention on con-text, on built environment, on the materiality of bodies tormented by 'every disease and every sickness' (4.23; 9.35) and afflicted by 'various diseases and pains' (with 4.24 listing demoniacs, epileptics and paralytics) in a way that alerts readers to the very specificity of these bodily afflictions, and of bodies speaking and listening.

These summary passages also reiterate that the ministry of Jesus, whether his words or his healing actions, take readers into the realm of power. The waters of the Jordan and the words of the heavenly voice authorized Jesus (3.16-17), and it is as authorised teacher and preacher in the synagogues of Galilee that he proclaims the good news (*euanggelion*) of the *basileia* (see 3.2 and 4.17). This proclamation takes place, however, in a context of Galilee/Syria, a region that belongs within the political realm of the Roman empire. Power and contesting/contested power, functioning vertically and horizontally, are never far from the unfolding story of a new *basileia* that is at hand. This will be evident in the ethic of this new *basileia* that Jesus preaches from the mountaintop in Matthew 5–7.

At the outset, therefore, it is clear in this section of the Matthean Gospel, framed and informed by 4.23 and 9.35, that there is an integration of the cultural with the material in the ecological texture of the text. To read the proclamation of Jesus in Matthew 5–7, the context for the beatitudes, in a way that recognizes such integration calls for a significant shift to an ecological hermeneutic. This is in response to the nature/culture divide that constitutes one of the dualisms within the ideology of mastery which feminists, post-colonial critics and a growing number of ecological thinkers, writers and ethicists critique. It is only as a result of such a shift that humans recognize themselves as members of the 'ecological community'. This means that environmental justice, social justice and economic justice are intimately interrelated. This is not simply adding ecology to already existing reading paradigms but significantly shifting one's way of thinking. It returns us, therefore, to the ecological hermeneutic outlined above. Inherent in this is the recognition that reading ecologically is reading an ancient text with new eyes. This new reading will be shaped and formed by the rich intertexture within the text. Along one axis of intertexture will be the work of ecological ethicists, scientists and theologians which folds back into the text's intertexture. Along the other axis will be the encoding of ancient texts together with social, cultural and ecological traces of the text's con-texts.

Matthew 5.1 opens very explicitly with Jesus 'seeing' the crowds and going up the mountain. He is situated intimately in a more than human con-text, described in relation to his own sensory activity of 'seeing' the crowds (5.1 and 4.25) and his going up the material location of 'the mountain'. There he sits down, presumably on the ground or on a rock or stone and a group called 'disciples', a group not previously named in this way in the Gospel, comes to him and he relates to them bodily as well as socially, opening his mouth and teaching them.

The sensory activity of seeing (5.1) links Jesus by way of awareness to the crowds who are following him (4.25). The narrator does not explicitly locate the crowds in 5.1 in relation to the subsequent phrase that describes Jesus' going up the mountain. However, the concluding verses of the teaching of Jesus (7.28-29) correct this lacuna, making it clear to the reader that the crowds have been recipients of Jesus' teaching. Also, the narrative does not identify the 'mountain'; nor does it give details of what would have been a difficult process of getting not only Jesus but also disciples and crowds up a 'very high' mountain, such as the one identified in 4.8 and 17.1. Rather the term 'mountain' is only used here in a way to recognize the locational and geographical relativity of what is called a 'mountain'. Hence Jesus may be characterized as going up an incline that provided him with a place from which to preach and teach. In such a way, the reader encounters the initial geographical or material features of this reference. In addition, 'mountain' functions symbolically within the Matthean Gospel (see the many occurrences in 4.8; 5.1, 14; 8.1; 14.23; 15.29; 17.1, 9, 20; 18.12; 21.1, 21; 24.3, 16; 26.30; 28.16) with a range of meanings, as we will explore below. The very explicit emphasis on material location might function to open up potential for new meaning when read ecologically.

Intertextually, mountains are places of encounter with God for Abraham (Gen. 22.2-19), for Elijah (1 Kgs 19.8-18) and for Moses (Exod. 19.1-6). The mountain is also the place from which Israel receives God's covenantal law (Exod. 19.17-20; 24.12-18; 32.15-19; 34.1-9). The placing of Jesus 'on the mountain' authorizes him for teaching, a teaching that comes from his experience of encountering the divine or the holy, the one who is with the Earth community in Jesus (1.23) and is, therefore, with all the material and social actors who constitute this scene.

Jesus' bodily placement—sitting—further emphasizes his symbolic association with Moses and also the rabbinic teachers in his religious tradition. The phrase that follows, 'he opened his mouth', is not common in Matthew's Gospel (only 5.2; and 13.35, which cites Ps. 78.2). The strongest intertextuality is with the wisdom tradition where it is linked with the justice or righteousness of the one who 'opens the mouth' for the 'rights of the destitute' (Prov. 31.8) or defends the 'rights of the poor and needy' (Prov. 31.9). The material, the social and the symbolic intersect in this opening verse to characterize Jesus the teacher/preacher. The introduction to Jesus' teaching (5.1-2) concludes with the words 'and he taught them', thus further identifying him with Sophia/Wisdom and enabling male and female metaphors to come together with reference to the materiality of Jesus' human body to play inclusively in this intertextual characterization of Jesus who begins to preach/teach.

The first word that the listeners hear from the opened mouth of Jesus is *makarioi*—that is, 'fortunate', 'happy', 'privileged' or 'blessed'. Indeed, this same word is repeated eight more times as Jesus begins his first explicit preaching of the *basileia* of the heavens/sky (4.17). The first eight repetitions are followed by the third person plural article *hoi* ('blessed/happy/privileged *the*…'), while the ninth or last repetition is followed by the second person plural verb, *este*, that distinguishes it from the previous set of eight ('blessed/happy/privileged are *you*'). These proclamations that open Jesus' teaching describe God's *basileia* as already present, a presence that an ecological reader locates in the Earth community in which God is present in the person of Jesus (1.23). This is also made evident in the inner texture of the text in that the phrase 'theirs is the *basileia* of the heavens' frames the first eight proclamations (5.3b, 10b).

Intertextually, *makarioi* evokes the repeated affirmation by the psalmists of those who are in right relationship with God (Pss. 1.1; 32.1-2; 34.8; 40.4; 41.1; 65.4; 84.4-5, 12; 89.15; 94.12; 128.1; 146.5) and do what is right and just (Pss. 106.3; 119.1, 2). It also echoes the proclamation of the sages in relation to those who are wise and live the wisdom of Sophia (Prov. 3.13; 8.34; Sir. 14.1, 2; 14.20; 31.8; 34.17; 50.28). Such intertextuality highlights the profound anthropocentrism of these *makarioi* proclamations, as they seem to be focused on divine gifting and human virtues. Indeed, they would seem to confirm the charge that the biblical text is irredeemable from an ecological perspective. For the contemporary ecological reader, however, explorations of the ecological texture and the intertextuality emerging from dialogue with contemporary ecological ethics and theology render it possible to read the beatitudes anew.

Those first proclaimed *makarioi* are the 'poor in spirit' (Mt. 5.3). This particular phrase evokes little intertextually in that it occurs nowhere in the Jewish scriptures in this way nor, Hans Dieter Betz claims, in the Greek language (Betz 1995: 113). Betz does, however, point to two potential intertexts that he suggests capture the 'blessed condition' of being 'poor in spirit'. One such text is Sir. 40.1-11 that recognizes that all living beings return to the earth. A second is Isa. 40.6-8 that likens humans to grass as both wither and fade. Each of these intertexts emphasizes the materiality that all Earth's constituents share. Betz recognizes humility, 'a virtue highly praised in antiquity' (1995: 116), as corresponding to being poor in spirit. But such humility, such recognition of what the human person shares with all Earth constituents, is not only an ancient virtue to be named as blessed or favoured. It is recognized by James Nash, contemporary environmental theologian and ethicist, as being among our contemporary ecological virtues (1991: 66-67, 156-57). We can bring Nash's exploration of this ecological virtue of humility into dialogue, in the intertexture of Mt. 5.3, with Sirach and Isaiah's recognition of the life potential and life fragility that all beings share in the more than human community. This leads to a recognition that 'the poor in spirit' know who they are in the simplicity of their being, which is gift, and how they are in relation to all Earth's others.

Such humility can be likened to the self-emptying of the God who identifies with humanity, as in Phil. 2.3-11. We would extend this divine identification with humanity to include all Earth beings with whom the self-emptying one shares life. Similarly, the humility that we are associating with Jesus' affirmation of the 'poor in spirit' from an ecological perspective entails a shift of focus from oneself as self- or human-centred to being Earth-centred. This can bring a recognition of otherness, which calls forth awe—an awe which a reader might imagine that Jesus the preacher recognized as he engaged with the habitat in which his mountain-side preaching platform was located, and an awe that his human listeners might have shared while recognizing in him the one in whom God was with the Earth community. Indeed, being poor in spirit as an ecological virtue enables relationship or identification within the more than human Earth community, an identification that expands the self and enables meaningful action on account of a vision that the Matthean Gospel calls the *basileia* of the heavens or skies.

In the second half of Mt. 5.3, Jesus gives the reason why the 'poor in spirit', those who recognize their self-emptying participation with all other beings in the more than human community, are proclaimed blessed, honoured or happy: theirs *is* the *basileia* of the heavens/sky. The proclamation of John (3.2) and of Jesus (4.17, 23), the *basileia* of the heavens/sky, is present to and in those who live in the right ordering of the Earth community. The metaphor carries in it the materiality of the *ouranois* (the 'heavens' or 'skies'), together with the galaxies, stars and heavenly entities that inhabit that world and are visible in the night sky. The Hellenistic worldview was geocentric (or Earth-centric) with the orbs of the moon and other planets circling earth. The metaphor is not, therefore, limited by one place or even one understanding of the universe (especially given the plural *ouranois*), but it gives place to Jesus' new social imaginary that he calls the *basileia* of the heavens. It is among those of the disciples of Jesus gathered around him who are named as 'poor in spirit', those who recognize their inter-connectedness with all Earth's constituents now and not just in some future time. It is in contrast to the *basileia* of Rome, in which political and military power-over facilitated and constituted their vision of the *pax Romana*, with little attention given to the relationship/s between the humans and other than humans who inhabited this *basileia*.

The second proclamation of 'honour' or 'blessing' is directed to those who mourn (5.4). Intertextually, the verb designates those who have lost someone or something that they hold dear (Gen. 23.2; 37.34; 50.3; 1 Sam. 15.35); but the sage also mourns his ignorance of Wisdom (Sir. 51.19) and, in Hos. 4.3, the land and all beings who live in it mourn as Earth's creatures vanish (cf. Isa. 33.9; Jer. 4.28; 12.4), and people also mourn the fate of Earth (Amos 8.8). Mourning accompanies the loss of right relationships in the Earth community and in that community's relationship with the divine. See in particular Isa. 61.2-3, which many scholars consider the key intertext of Mt. 5.4 and of which Carter says that 'they mourn or lament the destructive impact of imperial powers such as Babylon (and Rome) which oppress God's people' (2000: 132). Relationships have been out of order at designated points in Israel's unfolding story and mourning has been the response of those members of the Earth community, including the land and the living beings it supports who recognize this. It is all these who mourn that Jesus proclaims as 'blessed'. Such grief and mourning for broken Earth relationships characterize many today who work for ecological transformation; it also characterizes those Earth creatures who mourn the loss of companions from a species or habitat or whose kin have been wantonly destroyed by expansive human power. Some environmentalists draw attention to the significance of mourning and rituals of grief as habitats, trees, grasses, animals and many others disappear from our world, often at the hands of a range of 'imperial' human powers in rural and urban places, in nations and globally.

While mourning is recognized and affirmed as a significant moment in Jesus' proclamation of God's *basileia* dream, it is not to become a permanent mode of being. Rather, the second half of this second beatitude points to a future beyond mourning: namely, being comforted. In seeking to understand this comforting, one might imagine that many of the sixty-five occurrences of the verb *pentheō* ('to mourn') in the LXX (the Greek translation of the Hebrew Scriptures known as the Septuagint) would have been followed by *parakaleō* ('to comfort'). But not so. There are only four verses in which the two verbs occur together (Gen. 37.5; 1 Chron. 7.22; Sir. 48.24 and Isa. 61.2). One of these (Sir. 48.24) refers to the prophet Isaiah's comforting of the people of Zion while a second is in the prophetic words of Isa. 61.2-3. It is perhaps these verses that offer most to making meaning of Mt. 5.4b. In the *basileia* vision of God's dream for the Earth, transformation can and will happen. Those who mourn, including the land or earth, will be given 'a garland instead of ashes' and the 'oil of gladness instead of mourning' (Isa. 61.3). The rich diversity of life on land, in the sea and in the skies and the very Earth itself, all who have mourned will be comforted when their diversity is able to flourish and be enhanced. Indeed, Isaiah says of all these metaphorically that they will be called 'oaks of righteousness' (61.3c). They become symbols of a restored right ordering; but more importantly, relationships within the entire more-than-human community are to be characterized by this right ordering (*dikaiosynē* or 'righteousness' weaves its way through the mountain proclamation, see Mt. 5.6, 10, 20; 6.1, 33). Nash captures a similar vision within the virtue of biodiversity, whose goal, he says, is 'a commitment to sustaining viable populations of all other species in healthy habitats until the end of their evolutionary time' (Nash 1991: 66).

Many have noted the close relationship between the first and third beatitude, between the poverty of spirit and the meekness that are honoured or proclaimed blessed. Intertextually, one notes that the NRSV translation of *praus* in the Old Testament is often 'humble' (Num. 12.3; Pss. 25.9; 34.2; 149.4; Zeph. 3.12; Zech. 9.9), the virtue associated above with the 'poor in spirit' and important for an ecological ethic. Extending this intertextuality, it can be demonstrated that meekness or gentleness was a prized virtue among the Greeks (Betz 1995: 124-25), carrying connotations of mildness or gentleness associated with true strength rather than arrogance and roughness. The most significant intertexture, however, is Psalm 37, in which the phrase 'shall inherit the earth' occurs five times; moreover, 'the meek' are named in Ps. 37.11 as those who will so inherit. Attentiveness to the ecological texture of Mt. 5.5 raises the question as to whether, subsequent to the biblical inclusion of the land and Earth's others among those who mourn, the 'meek' might also include the other than human. The relationality or sociality inherent in those honoured or blessed in these beatitudes may be able to be extended beyond the confines of the human community.

We turn now to a brief intertextual analysis of Mt. 5.5 in relation to Psalm 37, especially Ps. 37.11 ('But the meek shall inherit the land and delight themselves in abundant prosperity'). The psalm belongs to an ancient wisdom tradition that interprets the world in a dualistic way: the righteous inherit the earth while the wicked are 'cut off' (this is particularly evident in Ps. 37.25, 28b-29). The ecological reader will bring a hermeneutic of suspicion to such structures of power inherent in the socio-political texture of this text as well as that of Mt. 5.5. Land or earth (*gē*) is associated with power and possession, and inheriting the land/earth can very easily be locked into such a system in a way that constructs the land as an object to be inherited or possessed.

How then might Jesus' reference to inheriting the land be reconfigured in reading the ecological texture of the Matthean text? First, earth/land can be understood in its materiality and sociality. It is not simply dirt or ground; we now know that land/earth is rich with diversity and relationality. Within Israel's biblical tradition, land belongs to God, as the psalmist sings (Ps. 24.1). It was gifted to Israel as an inheritance (Num. 26.53; Ps. 105.11); Israel's task is to till it and keep it (Gen. 2.15), to engage relationally with it. An ecological reader will also be conscious of—and bring a hermeneutics of suspicion to—the alternate tradition of Gen. 1.26 of human dominion over all the other Earth creatures. Israel's history was fraught with abuse of land by those among them who accumulated ownership to enhance power; it was also fraught with loss of the land. First-century Galilee was no exception. The Matthean phrase 'inherit the earth' encodes in its social and cultural texture the loss of land by small landholders to the gradual process of wealthy owners, Jewish or Roman, gaining more and more land at the expense of the small farmers who were often overtaxed. This beatitude holds out a hope and a vision that the power of imperial acquisition might be reversed and that land might be accessible to all to sustain life.

Continuing the exploration of Psalm 37 and Mt. 5.5 intertextually, one finds that the psalm contrasts the wicked or wrongdoers with those who do good. This latter group is named in different ways, one of them being 'meek' (Ps. 37.11). Those who shall 'inherit the earth' are the ones who wait for God (Ps. 37.9), who are blessed by God (Ps. 37.22), the righteous (Ps. 37.29), and the one who is exhorted to wait for God and keep God's ways. Each of these phrases could describe the meek as they function interactively in the psalm. While each of the groups who will inherit the earth are named differently, the group repeatedly identified with 'doing good' in this psalm are the *dikaioi* or 'the righteous' (Ps. 37.12, 16, 17, 21, 25, 29, 30, 32, 39). Inheriting the earth in Mt. 5.5 can be understood, therefore, as being righteous, living according to the right ordering of the entire Earth and all its constituent beings. The beatitude honours those who engage in right acting, right living in relation to Earth, not from a position of arrogance but from humble right relationship.

We have already seen that righteousness weaves through the beatitudes, playing within the intertexture of 5.5. It becomes explicit in the fourth beatitude (5.6), when those who hunger and thirst for that righteousness are proclaimed blessed. This interweaving and structuring for meaning characterizes the eight beatitudes. Righteousness (*dikaiosynē*) concludes the first four beatitudes (5.6); it is also a characteristic of the eighth beatitude that concludes the second group of four (5.10). Together with the entire framing of the eight beatitudes with the central Matthean theme of the '*basileia* of the heavens' in 5.3 and 5.10, these two thematics infuse each of the makarisms as each, in turn, nuances these key Matthean themes. One could say that at the heart of the *basileia* vision that Jesus preaches in Matthew is *dikaiosynē* or righteousness, envisaged in the multifaceted features of the beatitudes.

Righteousness is one factor within the repetitive texture of Matthew's Gospel. We have already seen it on the lips of Jesus assuring John of the right ordering of John's baptism of Jesus (3.15). It occurs five times in Jesus' mountain proclamation (5.6, 10, 20; 6.1, 33), and its final occurrence is in 21.32. It is within Jesus' initial preaching that it has most significance. An exploration of the rich intertextuality infusing the use of *dikaiosynē* in the Matthean text would take us far beyond the scope of this study. Just briefly, we note that in translation it is rendered as righteousness or justice (Isa. 9.7; 11.5), and that it is often linked with *krima* or 'justice', as in Isa. 9.7. It is God's desired ordering of all relationships and so is praised by psalmist and prophet in texts too numerous to mention. It is also the desire of the sages. Its centrality overflows in Ps. 85.10-13, where it is linked to other key attributes of God's relationship with the Earth community.

> Steadfast love and faithfulness will meet;
> righteousness (*dikaiosynē*) and peace will kiss each other.
> Faithfulness will spring up from the ground,
> and righteousness (*dikaiosynē*) will look down from the sky.
> God will give what is good,
> and our land (*hē gē*) will yield its increase.
> Righteousness (*dikaiosynē*) will go before God,
> and will make a path for God's steps.

This righteousness is characteristic of divine, human and Earth interrelationships. The Matthean Jesus calls blessed those who hunger and thirst for such righteousness or justice, who long for it and who strive to enact it. It is here that ecological and social justice meet and embrace. What this right ordering means explicitly will need to be worked out in each unique location and community, each habitat or ecosystem. It is in this way that those hungering and thirsting will be satisfied; when that goal is reached, the *basileia* of the heavens will have been realized. The vision must be enacted in the now toward a realization in a future that one can only imagine.

Jesus' naming of the honoured ones in the new *basileia* of the heavens does not, however, stop here at this climax point of the first four makarisms; it continues into 5.7-10, where the merciful, the pure in heart, the peacemakers and those persecuted on account of Jesus' vision of righteousness are named as blessed. This second group of four makarisms could be seen to be turning different lenses on 'righteousness'. This would be in keeping with Betz's claim that '[e]thically, righteousness is the standard for human conduct and therefore for all ethical thinking and action. Ethical awareness means continual self-examination with regard to the principle of righteousness' (1995: 130). We will examine these next beatitudes briefly for any further nuances that they add to this ecological reading of Jesus' opening proclamation from the mountain.

Intertextually, mercy is a manifestation of the divine in the Old Testament; it is rendered in a number of ways, but in particular as *rachamim* or womb-compassion. The metaphor is grounded in the corporeal. Like righteousness in Ps. 85.10-13 (see above), it intersects with a number of other divine manifestations that are less corporeal. In Exod. 33.19 and Isa. 30.18, God's womb-compassionate mercy is linked with God's graciousness and in Isaiah with God's justice. In Isa. 30.18, the reference to God's womb-compassion is followed by a makarism: blessed are those who wait for God. Isa. 49.13 identifies the suffering ones as those who call forth God's womb-compassion, and Isa. 54.10 extends further the web of manifestations of mercy to God's steadfastness and covenant of peace:

> For the mountains may depart
> and the hills be removed,
> but my steadfast love (*hesed/eleos*) shall not depart from you,
> and my covenant of peace shall not be removed,
> says the Lord, who has compassion (*rachamim/eleos*) on you.

The merciful whom Jesus proclaims honoured in Mt. 5.8 can be understood intertextually, therefore, as those who are moved with womb compassion, just as God is characterized metaphorically as being moved corporeally for the ones, the Earth beings, who suffer. This is an aspect captured in the repetitive texture of Matthew's Gospel when this womb compassionate mercy is contrasted with sacrifice (9.13; 12.7). It called for personal and economical engagement not only within but also across households as resources needed to be shared and Earth honoured for mercy to be enacted in first-century Galilee. That mercy creates an interactive spiral of relationships is captured in the future passive indicative of the verb *eleeō*: they—the merciful ones—shall be given mercy. Such a spiral speaks of the right relationship envisioned between and among all Earth's constituents and the divine.

For today's ecological reader, suffering is not confined to the human community. Earth itself and all its constituents suffer the ravages of industrialization, over farming, dumping of toxic waste, disregard for animals and other devastations. It calls forth the corporeal womb compassion that can create communities of compassion, Earth communities of compassion, in which mercy is given and received. Nash's ecological virtues of frugality and equity (1991: 65) may contribute to the establishment of such communities of compassion.

The honouring of the 'pure in heart' and the promise that they will *see* God continue to emphasize the corporeality of the dispositions or the ethics of the makarisms. We are aware that they are virtues associated with the human among Earth's constituents and hence a certain anthropocentrism remains in this ecological reading. However, the ecological interpretation of each beatitude to this point has opened up awareness of the human in interrelationship with other Earth constituents, with the materiality within Earth relationships and the call to a right ordering of these relationships. This beatitude continues the same tensive relationship.

The reference to the pure in 'heart' alerts readers to the corporeal within the inner texture of the narrative; this is made even more explicit in this verse, which proclaims the 'pure in heart' blessed and claims that they shall 'see' God. Intertextually, Pss. 24.4 and 73.1 evoke the pure in heart standing in God's holy place and God being good to those whose hearts are pure, pointing in different terms to the 'right ordering' which characterizes the first four beatitudes. Within the ecological texture of the text, the heart and the eyes, evoked in the seeing of God, function both corporeally as well as socioculturally. They point to a human disposition, a way of turning toward one's being as Earth creature in relation to the divine and to Earth and all its constituents. Denis Edwards captures this in a description of Jesus that echoes Mt. 1.23: 'when one of us in the human and creaturely community, Jesus of Nazareth, is so radically open to God, so one with God, …we rightly see him as God-with-us' (2010: 158). This beatitude seems to call for such an openness—to God, to one's own corporeality and to other Earth beings—so that we will see God because God is with-us, the Earth community not only in Jesus but also in those ecological interrelationships and tendencies that are 'radically open to God'—God with us, the Earth community.

Making peace in first-century Galilee draws into the ecological texture of Mt. 5.9 the *Pax Romana* and Rome's subjection of all peoples in its vast empire. In Warren Carter's reading of this text, Rome makes peace by gathering into its fold the ruling classes of their occupied territories so resistance can be quickly quelled (Carter 2000: 135). This is not the peace that Jesus honours. Rather, the peacemakers he calls blessed are members of God's household, indeed the'sons' of that household. The ecological reader needs, therefore, to extend a significant hermeneutics of suspicion to the gendering of these householders as sons or male, as well as to the type of peace proposed in the context of empire.

As we have come to expect, however, a study of 5.9 intertextually can yield further insights. The *shalom* or peace of God permeates the Old

Testament, but there is just one use of the term 'peacemaker' and that is in Prov. 10.10, which yields little. Psalm 72, however, images the ideal king. As with the *pax Romana*, the dominion of this ideal king within the context of hierarchical structures needs to be approached with suspicion (Psalm 72/Ps. 71.8-11). That having been accomplished, the psalm praises those dispositions that make for an ideal *oikoumenos* or household of the world (Psalm 72/Ps. 71.8), dispositions that we can extend from the ideal king to the ideal members of the *oikoumenos* of God, the universe. As with the beatitudes, *dikaiosynē* is prominent (Psalm 72/Ps. 71.1, 2, 3, 7). In vv. 3 and 7, *eirēnē* ('peace') and *dikaiosynē* ('righteousness' or 'justice') occur together. The psalmist draws Earth's others into the vision of peace and justice (vv. 6 and 16), where they too would flourish in the right relationships of the ideal society: rain falls on the mown grass, showers water the earth, grain and fruit will be in abundance. Likewise, people too will flourish. These are the right relationships created by those who make ecological peace.

We have seen how the values, the ethical disposition and actions honoured in the opening proclamation of Jesus from the mountain are interwoven into an artfully constructed piece through which *dikaiosynē* ('righteousness') and the *basileia* of the heavens are threaded. These threads come together in the last of the eight benedictions: blessed are those persecuted on account of righteousness, because theirs is the *basileia* of the heavens (Mt. 5.10). As we have seen, any one of the features named blessed could be read and understood in relation to righteousness, the right ordering or justice that is of God. This is proclaimed in Jesus' vision of the *basileia* or the heavens/sky and can be extended and read ecologically.

Similarly, any one of the beatitudes or their combination practiced or enacted could bring about persecution. This summary beatitude indicates that these virtues or dispositions are not pious hopes but they are to be enacted in the face of the opposition which they will draw, as they did in the past for the prophets and the wise ones of old (5.12; Wis. 2.12-20). These final verses (Mt. 5.10–12) may well encode experiences of the followers of Jesus and/or of the Matthean community in Galilee or Galilee/Syria of the first century. They also function similarly for the contemporary ecological reader—one who is attentive to the ecological texture of the Matthean text and to the challenge an ecological reading provides in front of the text, as well as engaged in the ecological issues of today's world to bring together ecological, social and economic justice.

Conclusion

There is much more that could be said in relation to an ecological reading of the Matthean beatitudes. Suffice here to draw your attention again to the interweaving of an ecological hermeneutic with a nuanced socio-rhetorical methodology. The reading that emerges yields new meaning in front of the text, but also invites readers to new considerations of the text's intertextuality and its ecological texture that can inform a range of Matthean readers and readings.

Conclusion

As you come now to the end of this Guide to the Gospel according to Matthew, with its central programmatic of the *basileia* of the heavens near at hand and its frame of the presence of divinity and of the risen Jesus with the Earth community (1.23 and 28.20), it is our hope that you have come to know this particular Gospel text, its characters and its storyline in their particularity. We also hope that you have now met some of the key scholars who seek, in a variety of ways, to uncover the meaning of this text.

Another feature of this Guide has been an opening up of the range of ways in which scholars read the Matthean text. These are rich and varied at this point in time, so it is important in reading scholarly works and undertaking your own interpretation of the text to be aware of the particular interpretive lens or lenses through which the text is being read and the methodological tools that are being used. Each of these, especially in their interconnectedness, shape the meaning one claims for this text: the Gospel according to Matthew.

BIBLIOGRAPHY

All biblical references are from the New Revised Standard Version (NRSV) of the Bible.

Anderson, Janice Capel

1995 'Life on the Mississippi: New Currents in Matthean Scholarship', *CRBS* 3: 169-218.

2001 'Matthew: Gender and Reading', in Levine (2001), pp. 25-51.

Anderson, Janice Capel, and Stephen D. Moore

2003 'Matthew and Masculinity', in Moore and Anderson (2003), pp. 67-92.

Beaton, Richard

2002 *Isaiah's Christ in Matthew's Gospel* (SNTSMS, 123; Cambridge: Cambridge University Press).

Bernabé, Carmen

2003 'Of Eunuchs and Predators: Matthew 19:1-12 in a Cultural Context', *BTB* 3: 128-34.

Betz, Hans Dieter

1995 *The Sermon on the Mount: A Commentary on the Sermon on the Mount, Including the Sermon on the Plain (Matthew 5:3–7:27 and Luke 6:20-49)* (Hermeneia; Minneapolis, MN: Fortress Press).

Bohache, Thomas

2006 'Matthew', in *The Queer Bible Commentary* (ed. Deryn Guest, Robert E. Goss, Mona West and Thomas Bohach; London: SCM Press), pp. 487-516.

Byrne, Brendan

2004 *Lifting the Burden: Reading Matthew's Gospel in the Church Today* (Collegeville, MN: Liturgical Press).

Carter, Warren

2000 *Matthew and the Margins: A Socio-Political and Religious Reading* (JSNTSup, 204; Sheffield: Sheffield Academic Press).

2001 *Matthew and Empire: Initial Explorations* (Harrisburg, PA: Trinity Press International).

2006 *The Roman Empire and the New Testament: An Essential Guide* (Abingdon Essential Guides; Nashville, TN: Abingdon Press).

Carter, Warren, and John Paul Heil

1998 *Matthew's Parables: Audience-Oriented Perspectives* (CBQMS, 30; Washington, DC: The Catholic Biblical Association of America).

Chancey, Mark A.

2005 *Greco-Roman Culture and the Galilee of Jesus* (SNTSMS, 134; Cambridge: Cambridge University Press).

Cheney, Emily
1996 *She Can Read: Feminist Reading Strategies for Biblical Narrative* (Valley Forge, PA: Trinity Press International).

Code, Lorraine
2006 *Ecological Thinking: The Politics of Epistemic Location* (Studies in Feminist Philosophy; New York: Oxford University Press).

Cohen, Shaye J.D.
1991 'Menstruants and the Sacred in Judaism and Christianity', in *Women's History and Ancient History* (ed. Sarah B. Pomeroy; Chapel Hill, NC: University of North Carolina), pp. 273-99.

Conway, Colleen M.
2008 *Behold the Man: Jesus and Greco-Roman Masculinity* (Oxford: Oxford University Press).

Crosby, Michael
1998 *House of Disciples: Church, Economics, and Justice in Matthew* (Maryknoll, NY: Orbis Books).

Davies, W.D., and Dale C. Allison
1988–1997 *A Critical and Exegetical Commentary on the Gospel according to Saint Matthew* (3 vols.; Edinburgh: T. & T. Clark).

Deutsch, Celia
1996 *Lady Wisdom, Jesus, and the Sages: Metaphor and Social Context in Matthew's Gospel* (Valley Forge, PA: Trinity Press International).
2001 'Jesus as Wisdom: A Feminist Reading of Matthew's Wisdom Christology', in Levine (2001), pp. 88-113.

Dube, Musa W.
1996 'Readings of Semoya: Batswana Women's Interpretations of Matt 15:21-28', *Semeia* 73: 111-29.
2000 *Postcolonial Feminist Interpretation of the Bible* (St Louis, MO: Chalice Press).
2001 *Other Ways of Reading: African Women and the Bible* (Global Perspectives on Biblical Scholarship, 2; Atlanta: Society of Biblical Literature).

Dube, Musa W., and Rachel Angogo Kanyoro
2004 *Grant me Justice! : HIV/AIDS & Gender Readings of the Bible* (Pietermaritzburg, South Africa: Cluster Publications).

Duling, Dennis C.
2012 *A Marginal Scribe: Studies in the Gospel of Matthew in a Social-Scientific Perspective* (Eugene, OR: Cascade Books).

Edwards, Denis
2010 *How God Acts: Creation, Redemption, and Special Divine Action* (Minneapolis, MN: Fortress Press).

Elvey, Anne F.
2011 *The Matter of the Text: Material Engagements between Luke and the Five Senses* (Bible in the Modern World, 37; Sheffield: Sheffield Phoenix Press).

Evans, Craig A.
2012 *Matthew* (New Cambridge Bible Commentary; New York: Cambridge University Press).

Ewherido, Anthony O.
2006 *Matthew's Gospel and Judaism in the Late First Century C.E.: The Evidence from Matthew's Chapter on Parables (Matthew 13:1-52)* (Studies in Biblical Literature, 91; New York: Peter Lang).

Fiorenza, Elisabeth Schüssler
1994 *Jesus: Miriam's child, Sophia's Prophet: Critical Issues in Feminist Christology* (New York: Continuum).
Fonrobert, Charlotte
1997 'The Women with a Blood-Flow (Mark 5:24-34) Revisited: Menstrual Polemics in Christian Feminist Hermeneutics', in *Early Christian Interpretation of the Scriptures of Israel* (ed. Craig A. Evans and James A. Sanders; Sheffield: Sheffield Academic Press), pp. 121-40.
France, R.T.
2007 *The Gospel of Matthew* (NICNT; Grand Rapids, MI: Eerdmans).
Freyne, Seán
2004 *Jesus, a Jewish Galilean: A New Reading of the Jesus Story* (London: T. & T. Clark).
Gale, Aaron M.
2005 *Redefining Ancient Borders: The Jewish Scribal Framework of Matthew's Gospel* (New York: T. & T. Clark).
Garrow, A.J.P.
2004 *The Gospel of Matthew's Dependence on the Didache* (JSNTSup, 254; London: T. & T. Clark).
West, Gerald, and Musa W. Dube (eds.)
1997 *'Reading with': An Exploration of the Interface between Critical and Ordinary Readings* (Semeia, 73; Atlanta: Society of Biblical Literature).
Gleason, Maud W.
2003 'New Testament Masculinities', in Moore and Anderson (2003), pp. 325-28.
Hannan, Margaret
2006 *The Nature and Demands of the Sovereign Rule of God in the Gospel of Matthew* (LNTS, 308; New York: T. & T. Clark).
Hare, Douglas R.A.
1993 *Matthew* (Interpretation; Louisville, KY: John Knox Press).
Hood, Jason B.
2011 *The Messiah, his Brothers, and the Nations (Matthew 1.1-17)* (London: T. & T. Clark).
Horsley, Richard A.
1989 *The Liberation of Christmas: The Infancy Narratives in Social Context* (New York: Crossroad).
1996 *Archaeology, History, and Society in Galilee: The Social Context of Jesus and the Rabbis* (Valley Forge, PA: Trinity Press International).
Humphries-Brooks, Stephenson
2001 'The Canaanite Woman in Matthew', in Levine (2001), pp. 138-56.
Jackson, Glenna S.
2002 *Have Mercy on Me: The Story of the Canaanite Woman in Matthew 15:21-28* (JSNTSup, 228; London: Sheffield Academic Press).
Jennings, Theodore W., and Tat-siong Benny Liew
2004 'Mistaken Identities but Model Faith: Rereading the Centurion, the Chap, and the Christ in Matthew 8:5-13', *JBL* 123: 467-94.
Keener, Craig S.
1999 *A Commentary on the Gospel of Matthew* (Grand Rapids. MI: Eerdmans).
2009 *The Gospel of Matthew: A Socio-Rhetorical Commentary* (Grand Rapids, MI: Eerdmans).

Koperski, Veronica

2011 'The Many Faces of the Canaanite Woman in Matthew 15,21-28', in Senior (2011), pp. 525-36.

Lenski, Gerhard E.

1966 *Power and Privilege; A Theory of Social Stratification* (New York: McGraw–Hill).

Levine, Amy-Jill

2001a 'Introduction', in Levine (2001), pp. 13-23.

2001b 'Discharging Responsibility: Matthean Jesus, Biblical Law, and Hemorrhaging Woman', in Levine (2001), pp. 70-87.

2001c 'Matthew's Advice to a Divided Readership', in *The Gospel of Matthew in Current Study* (ed. David E. Aune; Grand Rapids, MI: Eerdmans), pp. 22-41.

Levine, Amy-Jill, with Marianne Blickenstaff (eds.)

2001 *A Feminist Companion to Matthew* (Feminist Companion to the New Testament and Early Christian Writings, 1; Sheffield: Sheffield Academic Press).

Longstaff, Thomas R.W.

2001 'What are Those Women Doing at the Tomb of Jesus? Perspectives on Matthew 28.1', in Levine (2001), pp. 196-204.

Love, Stuart L.

2009 *Jesus and Marginal Women: The Gospel of Matthew in Social-Scientific Perspective* (Matrix: The Bible in Mediterranean Context, 5; Eugene, OR: Cascade Books).

Mattila, Talvikki

2002 *Citizens of the Kingdom: Followers in Matthew from a Feminist Perspective* (Publications of the Finnish Exegetical Society, 83; Helsinki: Finnish Exegetical Society).

Moore, Stephen D., and Janice Capel Anderson

2003 *New Testament Masculinities* (Semeia, 45: Atlanta: Society of Biblical Literature).

Nash, James A.

1991 *Loving Nature: Ecological Integrity and Christian Responsibility* (Nashville, TN: Abingdon Press).

Neyrey, Jerome H.

1998 *Honor and Shame in the Gospel of Matthew* (Louisville, KY: Westminster/John Knox Press).

2003 'Jesus, Gender, and the Gospel of Matthew', in Moore and Anderson (2003), pp. 43-66.

Nolland, John

2005 *The Gospel of Matthew: A Commentary on the Greek Text* (NIGTC; Grand Rapids, MI: Eerdmans).

O'Day, Gail R.

2001 'Surprised by Faith: Jesus and the Canaanite Woman', in Levine (2001), pp. 114-25.

O'Leary, Anne M.

2006 *Matthew's Judaization of Mark: Examined in the Context of the Use of Sources in Graeco-Roman Antiquity* (LNTS, 323; London: T. & T. Clark).

Osiek, Carolyn

2001 'The Women at the Tomb: What are they Doing there?', in Levine (2001), pp. 205-20.

Overman, J. Andrew
1990 *Matthew's Gospel and Formative Judaism: The Social World of the Matthean Community* (Minneapolis, MN: Fortress Press).
Parambi, Baby
2003 *The Discipleship of Women in the Gospel According to Matthew: An Exegetical Theological Studies of Matt 27:51-56, 57-61; 28:1-10* (Rome: Editrice Pontificia Università Gregoriana).
Patte, Daniel, Monya A. Stubbs, Justin S. Ukpong and Revelation E. Velunta
2003 *The Gospel of Matthew: A Contextual Introduction for Group Study* (Nashville, TN: Abingdon Press).
Pennington, Jonathan T.
2007 *Heaven and Earth in the Gospel of Matthew* (NovTSup, 126; Leiden: Brill).
Powell, Mark Allan (ed.)
2009 *Methods for Matthew* (Cambridge: Cambridge University Press).
Pregeant, Russell
2004 *Matthew* (Chalice Commentaries for Today; St Louis, MO: Chalice Press).
Riches, John, and David C. Sim
2005 *The Gospel of Matthew in its Roman Imperial Context* (JSNTSup, 276; London: T. & T. Clark).
Riches, John
1996 *Matthew* (Sheffield: Sheffield Academic Press).
Robbins, Vernon K.
1996 *Exploring the Texture of Texts: A Guide to Socio-Rhetorical Interpretations* (Valley Forge, PA: Trinity Press International).
Rosenblatt, Marie-Eloise
2001 'Got into the Party after All: Women's Issues and the Five Foolish Virgins', in Levine (2001), pp. 171-95.
Saldarini, Anthony J.
1994 *Matthew's Christian-Jewish Community* (Chicago Studies in the History of Judaism; Chicago: University of Chicago Press).
Schaberg, Jane
2006 *The Illegitimacy of Jesus: A Feminist Theological Interpretation of the Infancy Narratives* (Sheffield: Sheffield Phoenix Press, expanded 20th anniversary edn).
Segovia, Fernando F., and R.S. Sugirtharajah (eds.)
2007 *A Postcolonial Commentary on the New Testament Writings* (The Bible and Postcolonialism; London: T. & T. Clark).
Segovia, Fernando F.
2009 'Postcolonial Criticism and the Gospel of Matthew', in Powell (2009), pp. 194-238.
Senior, Donald
1983 *What Are They Saying about Matthew?* (New York: Paulist Press).
1996 *What Are They Saying about Matthew?* (New York: Paulist Press, 2nd edn).
1998 *Matthew* (Abingdon New Testament Commentaries; Nashville, TN: Abingdon Press).
Senior, Donal (ed.)
2011 *The Gospel of Matthew at the Crossroads of Early Christianity* (BETL, 243; Leuven: Peeters).
Sheffield, Julian
2001 'The Father in the Gospel of Matthew', in Levine (2001), pp. 52-69.

Sim, David C.
1998 *The Gospel of Matthew and Christian Judaism: The History and Social Setting of the Matthean Community* (Studies of the New Testament and Its World; Edinburgh: T. & T. Clark).
Slee, Michelle
2003 *The Church in Antioch in the First Century CE: Communion and Conflict* (JSNTSup, 244. London: Sheffield Academic Press).
Thompson, William G.
1970 *Matthew's Advice to a Divided Community* (Rome: Biblical Institute Press).
Tuilier, André
2005 'Les charismatiques itinérants dans la Didachè et dans l'Évangile de Matthieu', in *Matthew and the Didache: Two Documents from the Same Jewish-Christian Milieu?* (ed. Huub van de Sandt. Assen: Royal Van Gorcum), pp. 157-69.
Vledder, Evert-Jan
1997 *Conflict in the Miracle Stories: A Socio-Exegetical Study of Matthew 8 and 9* (JSNTSup, 152; Sheffield: Sheffield Academic Press).
Wainwright, Elaine Mary
1991 *Towards a Feminist Critical Reading of the Gospel according to Matthew* (BZNW, 60; Berlin: de Gruyter).
1994 'The Gospel of Matthew', in *Searching the Scriptures*. II. *A Feminist Commentary* (ed. Elisabeth Schüssler Fiorenza; New York: Crossroads), pp. 635-77.
1998 *Shall We Look for Another? A Feminist Rereading of the Matthean Jesus* (Maryknoll, NY: Orbis Books).
2001 'Not without my Daughter: Gender and Demon Possession in Matthew 15.21-28', in Levine (2001), pp. 126-37.
2006 *Women Healing/Healing Women: The Genderization of Healing in Early Christianity* (London: Equinox).
2009a 'Feminist Criticism and the Gospel of Matthew', in Powell (2009), pp. 83-117.
2009b 'Land of the Kauri and the Long White Cloud: Beginning to Read Matthew 1–2 Ecologically', in *Postcolonial Interventions: Essays in Honor of R.S. Sugirtharajah* (ed. T.S.B. Liew; Sheffield: Sheffield Phoenix Press), pp. 332-46.
2010 'Place, Power and Potentiality: Reading Matthew 2:1-12 Ecologically', *ExpTim* 121: 159-67.
2011 'Beyond the Crossroads: Reading Matthew 13, 52 Ecologically into the Twenty-First Century', in Senior (2011), pp. 375-88.
2012a 'Hear Then the Parable of the Seed: Reading the Agrarian Parables of Matthew 13 Ecologically', in *The One Who Reads May Run: Essays in Honour of Edgar W. Conrad* (New York: T. & T. Clark), pp. 125-41.
2012 'Reading Matt 21:12-22 Ecologically'. *Australian Biblical Review* 60: 67-79.
2012b 'Images, Words and Stories: Exploring their Transformative Power in Reading Biblical Texts Ecologically', *BibInt* 20: 280-304.
2013 'Reading the Gospel of Matthew Ecologically in Oceania: Matthew 4:1-11 as Focal Text', in *Matthew* (ed. Nicole Wilkinson Duran and James P. Grimshaw; Minneapolis, MN: Fortress Press), pp. 255-70.

West, Gerald O., and Musa W. Dube
2000 *The Bible in Africa: Transactions, Trajectories, and Trends* (Leiden: Brill).
Willitts, Joel
2007 *Matthew's Messianic Shepherd-King: In Search of 'the Lost Sheep of the House of Israel'* (BZNW, 147; Berlin: de Gruyter).
Wilson, Alistair I.
2004 *When Will These Things Happen? A Study of Jesus as Judge in Matthew 21–25* (Paternoster Biblical Monographs; Carlisle: Paternoster Press).
Yamasaki, Gary
1998 *John the Baptist in Life and Death: Audience-Oriented Criticism of Matthew's Narrative* (JSNTSup, 167; Sheffield: Sheffield Academic Press).

Index of Subjects

Index of Authors